D0999725

GO FOR GOAL

GO FOR GOAL

Winning Drills and Exercises for Soccer

GEORGE FORD
Dexter School

JIM KANE

Allyn and Bacon, Inc.

Boston   London   Sydney   Toronto

Library of Congress Cataloging in Publication Data

Ford, George, 1937–
  Go for goal.

  Includes index.
    1. Soccer—Training. 2. Soccer—Coaching. I. Kane,
Jim, 1944–   . II. Title.
GV943.9.T7F67 1984   796.334   83-22303
ISBN 0-205-08065-0

Printed in the United States of America

10 9 8 7 6 5 4 3 2 1 88 87 86 85 84

About the Authors

George Ford has been playing and coaching soccer for over twenty years. He has been the Head Varsity Coach for Harvard University. He earned his B.S. degree from Rhode Island College and was awarded a Certification from the U.S. Soccer Federation Coaching School at Rollins College, Florida. George Ford has served as Head Coach at Bryant College, and at Woonsocket High School, both in Rhode Island. In addition, he has served on the national coaching staff as Director of the Region I Olympic Development Soccer Camp, and as director of various soccer camps throughout the country, and as a consultant to Hyde Athletic Industries. He is the author of *Basic Soccer: Strategies for Successful Player and Program Development,* also published by Allyn and Bacon.

Jim Kane is a freelance writer and editor. He resides on Martha's Vineyard, where he coaches youth soccer when he is not writing.

Contents

Preface

This book is intended for both the experienced coach and the beginner coach. With over one hundred and twenty basic drills and almost one hundred variations on the basic drills, even the most experienced coach will find many exercises to add to his own list of favorites. There are drills to reinforce player understanding both of the laws of the game and of the basic principles of play, drills for physical fitness, and fun games and exercises designed to stimulate player enthusiasm and bring variety to practice sessions.

Special features for the beginner coach include short explanations of the principles of play and suggested preseason training programs that provide detailed answers to the age-old question, "Now that I'm a coach, what do I do?"

The book includes drills for players of all ages and all levels of experience. As an organizational tool, each drill dealing with the laws of the game and the principles of play, as well as the fun games and exercises, begins by specifying the number of players to be included, appropriate player ages, playing area required, equipment necessary, and suggested duration of the drill. Such specifications allow the coach to plan his practices in advance in such a way as to individualize instruction as much as possible. Thus, for example, a coach may lead some beginning players through drills designed to familiarize them with the laws of the game, while an assistant coach works with more experienced players on drills to develop dribbling or ball control techniques.

Another special feature of the book involves the fitness exercises in Section 3. This section includes stretching exercises for flexibility, as well as exercises for power and endurance and for speed and strength. For each of these drills, the unit of time of the exercise and the number of repetitions are specified, as well as recovery exercises designed to avoid muscle problems that commonly result from fitness exercises.

It is hoped that coaches will incorporate the various types of drills into their practices in order to develop players who are not only fit, technically proficient, and tactically "savvy," but also players who maintain their enthusiasm for the game of soccer.

GO FOR GOAL

1

Drills to Reinforce Selected Laws of the Game

Every coach and player must understand the laws of the game and compete within the spirit of the laws. Unfortunately, beginner coaches and players have so much to learn about soccer that its most important aspect, its laws, are often learned over a period of years and, in many instances, after some embarrassing experiences.

This section is meant to familiarize the beginner coach and player with the laws that most commonly come into play *during a match*. (Laws governing types of footwear, the referees, ball specifications, etc., have been omitted.) Where appropriate, brief explanations of the laws precede the actual drills, which are offered as a means of reinforcing the players' understanding of the laws.

A successful team is one that can make the laws of the game work to its advantage.

FIELD OF PLAY

Players: All players
Playing Area: Full field
Equipment: One soccer ball per player plus one for the coach
Time: Not to exceed fifteen minutes; repeat from day to day as necessary

The coach assembles all players in the center circle. Each player has a ball. The players follow the coach, dribbling along the center line and around the field—

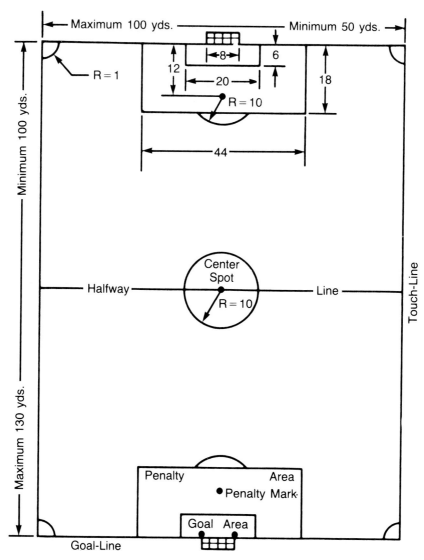

Provided the principles of the laws are maintained they may be modified by local associations to suit different age groups.

FIGURE 1-1   The field of play

down one touchline, across the goal line, down the other touchline, etc. (See Figure 1-1 for field markings.) The coach calls out the names of the lines as they progress back toward the center circle, while at the same time reinforcing dribbling technique along the way by instructing the players to keep the ball on the line, stop/start, pull the ball back and forth across the line, etc.

Once back at the center circle, the players continue to work on dribbling technique. The coach then gives the following hand signals: one finger raised, meaning to dribble the ball at speed, bringing it to rest on either touchline before returning to the center circle; two fingers raised, meaning to dribble at speed, rest the ball on either goal line, and return.

After continued dribbling practice, the coach leads the players to the top of the penalty area box (the side toward the center circle). The players dribble around the perimeter of the penalty area (including the retaining arc, if marked), before continuing dribbling practice within the area. The coach again gives signals: one finger, meaning to dribble to, and place the ball on, the top line of the penalty area; two fingers, meaning to dribble to either side of the penalty area; three fingers, meaning to place the ball on the retaining arc.

The exercise then continues in the same manner, substituting the goal area for the penalty area.

The players finally return to the center circle. Dribbling practice continues until the coach gives the following hand signals: one finger on either hand, meaning to dribble around the center circle; two fingers on the right (left) hand, meaning to dribble to the right (left) penalty area; three fingers on the right (left) hand, meaning to dribble to the right (left) goal area.

PLAYER POSITIONS

Players: All beginning players
Playing Area: Half-field
Equipment: One soccer ball per player; ten markers
Time: Six minutes

The coach places markers around the field to correspond to the positions of players *at the start of a game* (except for the goalkeeper). He assigns players to the markers, tells them the names of their positions, explaining that the markers indicate start-of-game positioning, and instructs them to observe the placement of teammates relative to themselves.

The players then assemble in the center circle and practice dribbling. On command, the players are to dribble to their respective markers and return to the center circle. Once back, they continue to dribble while the coach removes the markers. When the command is given again, the players are to find their positions without benefit of the markers.

The exercise should be repeated during the course of the season until each player has been assigned to each position. The coach should place the markers in two different ways: one to correspond to start of game on offense and one on defense, with the position of the two strikers varied accordingly.

Note: Figures 1-2 and 1-3 illustrate start-of-game positions on offense and defense, respectively, for the 4-2-4 alignment. Figure 1-4 illustrates start-of-game positions, on offense or defense, for the 4-3-3 alignment.

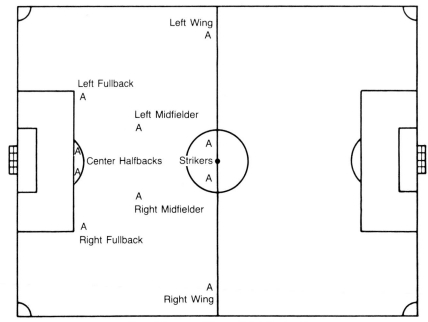

Start of Game on Offense (4-2-4 Alignment)

FIGURE 1-2

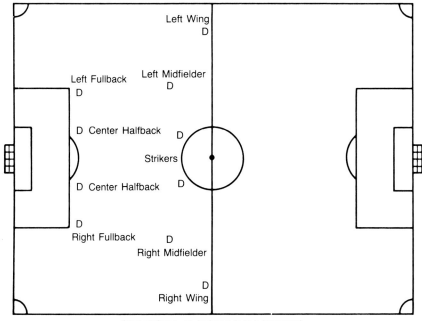

Start of Game on Defense (4-2-4 Alignment)

FIGURE 1-3

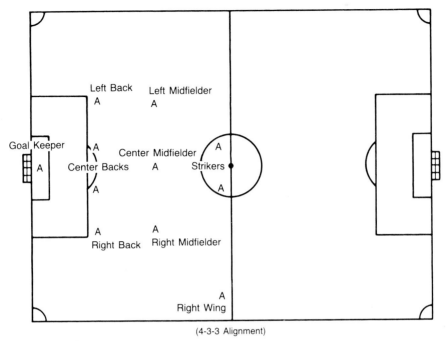

(4-3-3 Alignment)

FIGURE 1-4

START OF PLAY

The game shall be started (on the whistle) by a player taking a place kick (the ball must be stationary on the center spot) into the opponents' half of the field. The ball must travel one full revolution into the opposite side of the field before the game officially begins. The kicker may not play the ball a second time until it has been touched by another player from either team. At the start of the game, all players must be in their own half of the field, and the defenders must be at least ten yards from the ball. After each goal and after half time, the game is restarted in like manner.

In the event of injury or some other temporary suspension of play (occurring when the ball is in the field of play), which is not caused by any violation of the rules, the game is restarted with a drop ball (one bounce), either in the same area of the field as when the game was suspended or elsewhere at the referee's discretion.

Players: All players
Playing Area: Half-field
Equipment: Three soccer balls at most
Time: Ten minutes

The players are divided into two lines, which stand facing the goal. One line of players stands directly behind the center spot, the other approximately one yard to the side. The ball is placed on the center spot, as it would be for the start of play.

On the coach's command, the player immediately behind the ball passes it forward, making sure that it travels one full revolution beyond the center line. The first player in the other line receives the pass, and the two continue downfield, interpassing the ball. Once at the top of the penalty area, they pass the ball to the goalkeeper for gathering and distribution practice. The goalkeeper returns the ball to one of the two players, who then return along a touchline to the center circle. The two players then go to the back of the lines of players (each switching to a different line).

Once two players have progressed to the retaining arc, the next two players in line begin with another ball.

The exercise then continues with a small-sided game (six versus six) on a 40 x 30 yard grid centered on the center circle, with flags designating the goal placed the normal eight yards apart. Each time a goal is scored, the game restarts as per Law 8.

Variation 1

Two players are designated as defenders and one as a goalkeeper. The remaining players are divided into four groups and positioned as in Figure 1-5. The ball is placed on the center spot. (Note: the two defenders line up at the defensive side of the center circle, as they would for the start of play.)

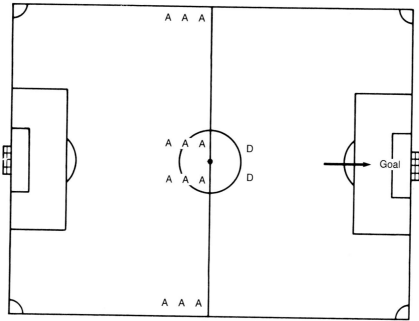

FIGURE 1-5

On the coach's command, the attacker directly behind the ball has the option of passing to the immediately supporting player or to either supporting winger. The four attackers then progress downfield, interpassing, and have a designated amount of time in which to shoot on goal (approximately fifteen seconds). The players then rotate positions—the original strikers become wingers, the wingers become defenders, the defenders become strikers.

Variation 2

The players assume positions as if they were ready to start play on offense. (See Figure 1-6). One ball is provided.

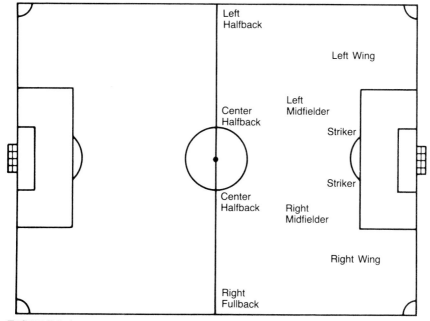

FIGURE 1-6

On the coach's command, the ball is played forward as in the normal start of play, and the players proceed downfield in unison, interpassing the ball. Any player receiving a pass must control the ball before passing it on to a player of his choice. The exercise continues until the wingers reach the top of the penalty area (at which point the fullbacks should be approximately at the center line, with the midfielders midway between the fullbacks and wingers). The wingers shoot on goal from the top of the penalty area.

The direction of play now reverses, with the fullbacks becoming wingers, etc.

METHODS OF SCORING

Players: All players
Playing Area: Full field
Equipment: Six soccer balls, eight markers, goal cages
Time: Ten minutes per part

Part 1

The players are divided into two teams, which line up in front of one goal at the retaining arc. Each team is provided with three soccer balls.

On the coach's command, the first player in each line dribbles the ball at speed to the top of the goal area, where he shoots on the empty net. He then retrieves the ball and lines up behind the other team.

Part 2

The exercise continues with small-sided games played on 20 x 25 yard grids that extend back from each goal area toward the center line. (See Figure 1-7). Goals are designated by markers placed two yards apart at each end of a grid.

For each grid, three attackers and two defenders are designated, with one defender appointed to guard the goal. If the two defenders win the ball over, they

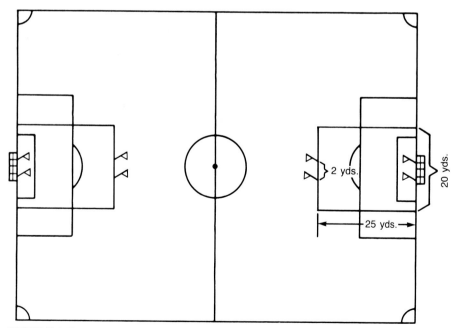

FIGURE 1-7

switch to the attack, being joined by one of the original attackers. The two remaining players now become defenders, again with one designated to guard the goal, such that the games are always played three versus two.

Variation 1

The players line up as in Part 1, above. The first player on each team rolls the ball with his hand toward the goal area, immediately chases, and shoots on the empty goal.

Variation 2

The players again line up as in Part 1. The first player on each team jogs toward the goal area, carrying the ball. At the top of the goal area, the player drops the ball and volleys it at the goal (shoots before the ball touches the ground).

Variation 3

One player is designated as goalkeeper. The remaining players are divided into two teams, which line up at the outside corners of the penalty area. (See Figure 1-8.) Approximately four soccer balls are provided to one of the teams. On the coach's command, a player dribbles the ball along the top of the penalty area (the

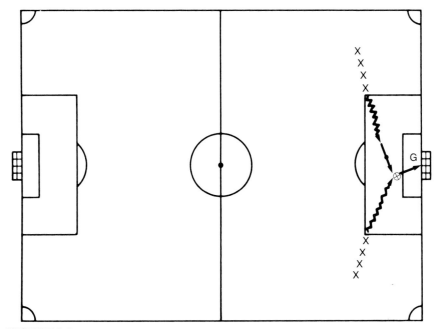

FIGURE 1-8

side toward the center circle) until reaching the retaining arc, where he passes the ball at an angle toward and through the penalty spot. At the moment the pass is made, the first player from the other team races to shoot on goal without first controlling the ball ("first-time shot on goal").

Variation 4

Two players are designated as "servers" and stand just outside the goalposts, each with three soccer balls. The remaining players are divided into two groups, which line up just outside the goal area, facing the goal and just to the inside of the goalposts. On the coach's command, each server tosses a ball underhand for the first player in line to head into the empty net. The shooter then retrieves the ball and becomes a server; the server goes to the back of the line on his side of the goal.

Variation 5

One player is designated as a goalkeeper, one as a server. The server stands just outside the goalposts. The remaining players line up at the top corner of the goal area, diagonally across from the server. On command, the server tosses the ball across the goal area, and the first player in line attempts to head it for a goal.

Variation 6

One player is designated as goalkeeper. The remaining players line up outside the penalty spot, facing the goal. The goalkeeper serves the ball to the first player in line, who attempts to head it for a goal.

Variation 7

A grid is marked off, thirty-six yards wide (centered on the goal) and eight yards deep. Four players are positioned in front of the goal and four behind, with the remaining players retrieving stray balls. Three soccer balls are provided. On the coach's command, the balls are shot through the open goal and returned, again through the goal, by the nearest player on the opposite side. No player may shoot within six yards of the goal (the depth of the goal area).

The game is continuous, with the depth of the grid adjusted to player strength. Balls are passed and returned through the goal using all parts of the body except the hands. The shooters and retrievers change roles intermittently.

PENALTY KICKS

A penalty kick is taken from the penalty spot. All players other than the kicker and opposing goalkeeper must stand outside the penalty area (which also includes the retaining arc) while the kick is taken.

The goalkeeper must stand on the goal line and may not move his feet until the ball has been kicked. Movement of the upper body is permitted. Should the shot rebound into the field of play, the kicker may not play the ball again until it has been touched by an opponent (in most cases, this will be the goalkeeper).

Players: All players
Playing Area: Both penalty areas
Equipment: Two soccer balls; four markers
Time: Part 1: ten minutes; Part 2: ten minutes; Part 3: twenty minutes

Part 1

A goalkeeper is assigned to each goal. The remaining players are divided into two groups and lined up outside the penalty areas, facing a soccer ball placed on the penalty spot. Each player in a group will shoot to score and then return the ball to one side of the penalty area; those who do not score go to the other side.

The exercise continues for as many rounds as are necessary to determine a winner from each end of the field. These two players will then play off against one another.

If the goalkeeper loses control of a shot, the kicker may follow his shot and try again before the goalie can control the ball, as per Law 14.

Part 2

A small-sided game (four versus four) is played within each penalty area, with flags placed one yard apart marking a goal at each end of the penalty area. The coach instructs the players that, on command, a designated player will shoot the ball on the regulation goal from the penalty spot. All players other than the kicker and goalkeeper must remain outside the penalty area until the shot is taken. As in Part 1, if the goalkeeper fails to control the shot, it is a live ball for attackers and defenders.

Part 3

The grids from Part 2 are doubled to equal two adjacent penalty areas at each end of the field. Two games are organized, each five versus five, with a goalkeeper designated for each of the four teams. The goals are regulation width.

Regular soccer rules are observed, with special emphasis on Law 12, so that if a player commits any of the nine infractions within his own penalty area, the opposing team is awarded a penalty kick, as per Law 14.

THROW-INS

A throw-in is awarded when the ball passes completely over a touchline, either on the ground or in the air. The team that last touched the ball shall lose possession via the throw-in. The ball must be thrown back into the field of play, in any direction, from the point where it crossed the touchline.

When making a throw-in, a player must hold the ball such that his hands form a 'W' with thumbs touching. The ball is taken back over the head until it rests on the back of the neck. The ball is thrown in making sure that the feet stay in contact with the ground at all times.

A goal may not be scored directly from a throw-in.

Players: All players
Playing Area: Full field
Equipment: As indicated
Time: As indicated

Part 1 (Time: three minutes. Equipment: one ball for each two players)

The players are paired into servers and receivers. Servers stand to the outside of one touchline, approximately five yards apart and each holding a ball. Receivers stand approximately ten yards infield, facing their partners.

On the coach's command, the servers execute a proper throw-in to their partners, who will control the ball and pass it back to the servers. After five throw-ins, the servers and receivers change positions.

Variation on Part 1 (Time: five minutes)

The players are divided into four groups, each with one designated receiver. For each group, the servers line up outside a touchline, facing infield. The receiver again stands approximately ten yards infield.

The receiver must control the ball before dribbling it back to the next server in line, who becomes the new receiver. The original receiver retires to the back of the line of servers.

Part 2 (Time: ten minutes. Equipment: three markers for each four players)

The players are divided into groups of four, composed of one server and three receivers. The receivers are positioned at markers. (See Figure 1-9). On the server's command, the receivers rotate positions as indicated in the figure, with the receiver in position #1 always proceeding clockwise to the corner of the penalty area. The server passes the ball to said corner so the ball and receiver arrive at the same time.

The exercise continues with the server throwing in to each receiver at each of the positions. The server will always follow his pass in order to support the player on the ball and go for a shot on goal.

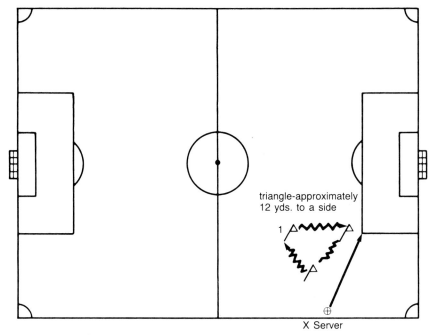

triangle-approximately
12 yds. to a side

1

X Server

FIGURE 1-9

Variation on Part 2

Two defenders are added to man-mark two of the receivers. The server throws in to the open area created by the movement of the receivers, again following his pass. The server and receivers then go for goal.

Part 3

A small-sided game (six versus six) is organized on grids marked off as per Figure 1-10 on page 14. Whenever the ball passes out of play, a throw-in will be taken as per Law 15.

GOAL KICKS

A goal kick is awarded to the defending team when an attacker causes the ball to pass completely over the goal line, either on the ground or in the air.

When a goal kick is awarded, the ball is placed within that half of the goal area nearest to where the ball went out of play. Any player may take the goal kick (usually the strongest kicker), and all opponents must stand outside the penalty

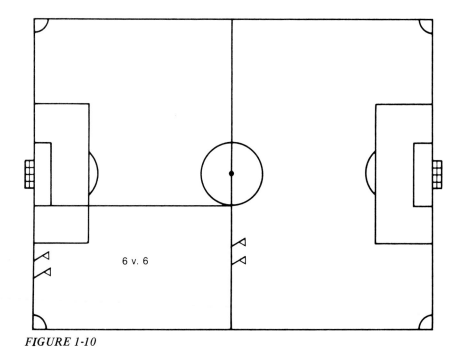

FIGURE 1-10

area until the kick is made. The ball must leave the penalty area before the game resumes.

If the kicker miskicks the ball, such that it does not leave the penalty area, he may not attempt to continue play with a second kick. In this case, the referee will award another kick, and a new kicker may be inserted, if desired.

Players: All players
Playing Area: Full field
Equipment: As indicated
Time: Six minutes per part

Part 1 (Equipment: one soccer ball,
two markers for each three groups)

The players are divided into groups, with no more than three players to a group. Three groups are then positioned at one corner of the field (see Figure 1-11), another three groups at another corner, etc.

At each corner of the field, group A lines up behind a marker placed midway between the touchline and the penalty, and midway between the goal line and the top of the penalty area. Group B lines up behind a marker placed approximately twelve yards upfield from the penalty area and in line with group A's marker.

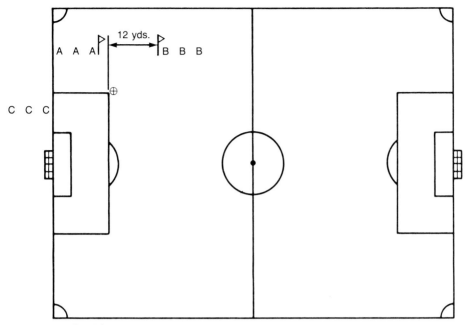

FIGURE 1-11

Group C lines up to the side of the goal. A ball is placed on the outside corner of the penalty area.

The first player in group C runs onto the ball and passes it to the first player in group A, who controls it before passing it on to the first player in group B. The group B player controls the ball and dribbles toward the goal to take a shot.

The exercise continues until each player has completed a round, i.e., has participated as a member of each of the three groups.

Variation on Part 1

Markers are placed as in Figure 1-12 on page 16. One player is stationed at each marker, and a goalkeeper and defender are designated.

On command, the goalkeeper will make a goal kick, as per Law 16, to any of his four supporting players, who will then attempt to make five consecutive passes under pressure from the defender. The players rotate positions when the five passes are completed or when the defender wins the ball over. Additional defenders may be assigned at the coach's discretion.

Part 2

Small-sided games (four versus four or five versus five) are played in the penalty areas. Goals at each end of the penalty area are designated by markers

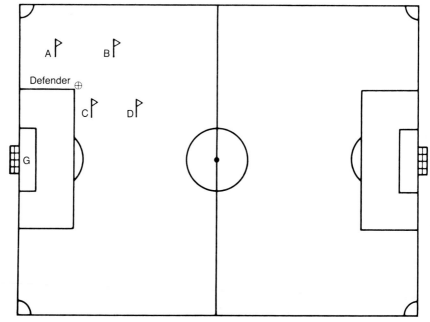

FIGURE 1-12

placed one yard apart. Whenever the ball passes over the regulation goal line or the touchline opposite same, a goal kick is awarded and all players (except the goalkeeper or a designated kicker on the defending team) must leave the penalty area, as per Rule 16. Once the goalkeeper has propelled the ball beyond the penalty area, the ball is brought back and play resumes.

CORNER KICKS

A corner kick is awarded to the attacking team when a defender causes the ball to pass completely over his own goal line, either in the air or on the ground.

The player taking a corner kick must place the ball within the quarter circle at the nearest corner flag. A goal may be scored directly from a corner kick, and the attackers cannot be off side at the time of the kick. Defending players must stand at least ten yards from the ball during the kick.

Players: All players
Playing Area: Four corners of the field
Equipment: Four soccer balls
Time: Six minutes per part

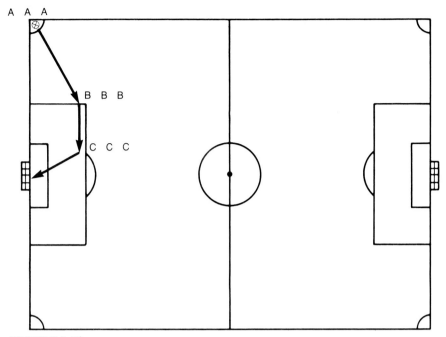

FIGURE 1-13

Part 1

The players are distributed as evenly as possible to the four corners of the field. At each corner, the players are divided into three groups and positioned as in Figure 1-13. A ball is placed within the corner arc.

The first player in group A passes the ball to the first player in group B, who controls and passes the ball in the direction of the penalty spot. The first player in group C moves onto the ball and shoots on goal. Player C then returns the ball to the corner arc and lines up behind players A (A goes to B, B goes to C).

Variation 1

Group C is moved to the corner of the goal area nearest group A. Player A again makes a corner kick to B, who passes to C, leading C toward the goal for a shot. The players rotate positions as above.

Variation 2

Groups B and C are repositioned to the two intersecting points of the retaining arc and the penalty area. (See Figure 1-14.) Group A is positioned as previously.

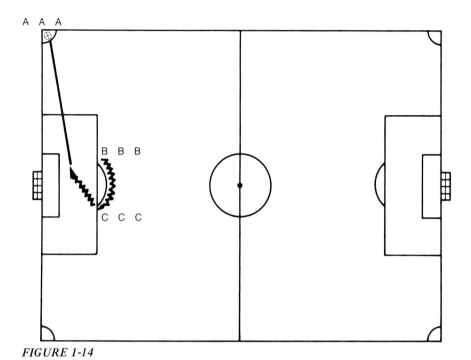

FIGURE 1-14

On A's command, player C sprints in the direction of the goalpost nearer player A, and B sprints around the retaining arc to player C's original position. Immediately after giving the command, player A kicks the ball to the front of the goal but outside the goal area, where C will shoot on goal. Any kick that passes behind or over C will be taken by player B, who will then shoot on goal.

Part 2

A small-sided game (five versus three plus two goalkeepers) is played on a grid of 20 x 30 yards (one game at each end of the field). One goal is established on the regular goal line, consisting of a single marker (G1 in Figure 1-15). To score, players A must strike the marker with the ball. G2 consists of two markers placed six yards apart. Players B score in the usual fashion.

Any ball passing over a goal line after last being touched by a defender will result in a corner kick, taken at the regulation corner arc. For corner kicks, all players will assume the normal offensive and defensive positions relative to the regular goal (i.e., the goalkeeper makes sure his fullbacks are positioned to the inside of the goalposts and the remaining defender man-marks the nearest attacker in front of the goal). The game restarts as per Law 17 with the attacking team attempting to score on goal.

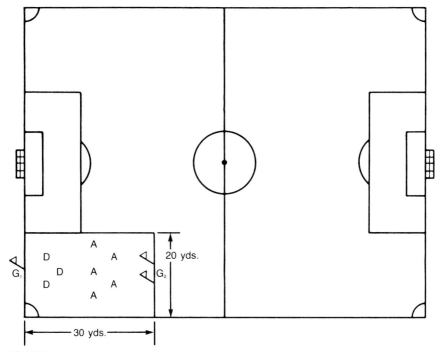

FIGURE 1-15

After each corner kick, resulting in either a shot on goal or an interception by the defenders, the game will resume within the grid, with players rotating between the two teams.

2

Drills to Reinforce the Principles of Play

Success in soccer is the result of a combination of factors: the will to win, good technique and, most importantly, an understanding and ability to apply the principles of play. Although goals scored during a match are the results of individual player technique and flair, the *situation* that allows the shot on goal most often results from the offensive team's application of the principles of attack as situations develop. Conversely, shots on goal are prevented by the defending team's application of the principles of defense.

By international standards, much recent progress has been made in the U.S. with regard to player fitness, technique, and tactical development. However, there is still much to be achieved relative to player understanding of the basic principles. In other words, players must learn to "read" the game—they must recognize their opponents' changing tactical deployments during the match and must learn to exploit the opponents' weaknesses and guard against their strengths.

The reader will note that the majority of the drills presented in this section are applicable to more experienced players, since most six to ten-year-old players must concentrate on the laws of the game and development of basic skills. For the somewhat older players, the coach is encouraged to select drills based upon his observations of individual player and team weaknesses. When presenting the following drills, a short explanation at the outset and a walk-through will prove invaluable.

Above all, it is important for the coach to remember that his players are basically on their own during a match. Thus the player who cannot read the game will be lost when facing an opponent who can.

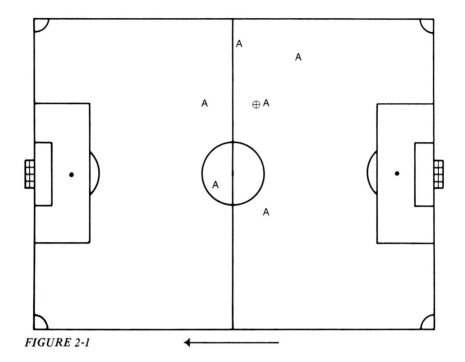

FIGURE 2-1

DEPTH IN ATTACK

In soccer, the term "depth" means support. Supporting players must be within passing range of the ball carrier and must be arrayed such that they can receive, control, and interpass the ball. Figure 2-1 illustrates proper depth in attack. The ball carrier is well supported by five of his teammates, allowing him a full range of passing opportunities and making the job of the defenders more difficult. The two most common violations of the principle of depth in attack are described below.

The first common violation occurs when players stand in a straight line across the field or run for the opponents' goal in a straight line. Such an error limits the ball carrier's options and makes it easier for the defenders to tackle the ball carrier, to intercept the ball, or to trap an attacker off side. Figure 2-2 illustrates this classic case of lack of depth in attack. The supporting players are standing "flat," i.e., in a straight line across the field. The only conceivably worse formation would be if the ball carrier were also part of this straight-line formation.

The second common violation of the principle of depth is illustrated in Figure 2-3, in which the forward players are charging toward the opponents' goal and away from the ball carrier. In this case, the ball carrier must power the ball over or through the defenders and hope that his teammates will reach the ball before the goalkeeper can gather it in or before it passes over the goal line. For the ball carrier, this is the equivalent of playing a golf hole where the green is approached through a series

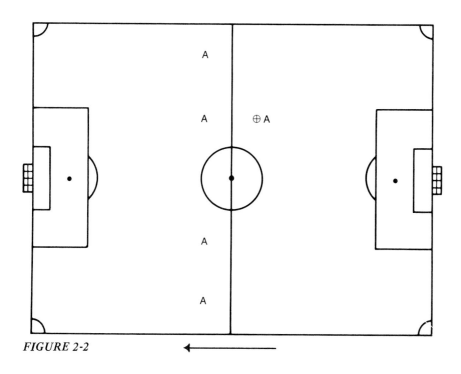

FIGURE 2-2

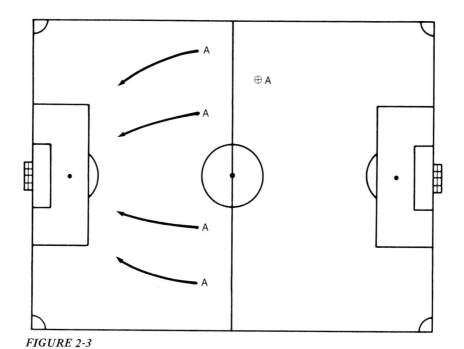

FIGURE 2-3

of traps, with a pond beyond the green and an antagonist deployed on the green to steal the ball. This situation also leads very often to an offside violation.

When players maintain proper field position, lines can be drawn between each combination of three players to form a series of interlocking triangles, with at least three players supporting the ball carrier. The following drills are offered to accustom players to maintaining such positioning.

Players: In groups of four
Ages: Ten and older
Playing Area: Center circle or similar area
Equipment: One soccer ball and four markers per group
Time: Nine minutes

Four markers are placed around the circumference of the center circle (or similar area), roughly equidistant from one another. The players are divided into groups of four, three attackers and one defender. The three attackers are stationed at the markers, leaving one marker unattended. The defender stands within the circle. One attacker has a soccer ball at his feet.

The players are instructed that each time an attacker passes the ball to a supporting player, he is to sprint to the unattended marker. The defender will attempt to intercept the pass.

On the coach's command, the attackers pass the ball in any direction, trying to complete as many successful passes as possible in the allotted time. Should the defender intercept a pass, the ball is immediately returned to the attackers, who begin again. After three stints of twenty to thirty-five seconds, the defender will change roles with one of the attackers.

Variation

The attackers play one-touch soccer.

Players: In groups of three
Ages: Ten and older
Playing Area: 10 x 10 yard grids along one touchline
Equipment: One soccer ball per group and sufficient markers
Time: Five minutes

For each group of three players, a grid of 10 x 10 yards is established, with the touchline comprising one side of the grid. Two attackers and one defender are designated for each group. The two attackers stand diagonally across from one another at opposite corners of the grid, one with a ball at his feet. The defender stands at either unoccupied corner.

On the coach's command, the attacker without the ball and the defender leave their corners, and the two attackers begin passing the ball. Five consecutive passes will constitute a goal. The attackers may move anywhere within the grid. The defender scores a goal by intercepting a pass or by tagging an attacker while the attacker is in possession of the ball.

When the attackers complete five passes, or when the defender intercepts the ball or tags the ball carrier, the players assume their original positions and the game resumes immediately. After three stints of twenty to thirty-five seconds, the defender changes roles with one of the attackers.

Variation 1

The attacking players score goals by passing the ball back and forth until one attacker is in a position to place the ball, with his foot, on any of the four grid lines. In this instance, the defender may score only by intercepting a pass or by tackling the ball away from an attacker.

Variation 2

While in their starting positions, the attacker with the ball throws it under-hand or makes a regulation throw-in diagonally across the grid to his teammate, who will bring the ball under control. The method of control is determined by the coach. The two attackers then play keep-away from the defender.

Players: In groups of three
Ages: Twelve and older
Playing Area: 10 x 20 yard grids
Equipment: One ball and four markers per group
Time: Four minutes

For each group of three, four markers are placed to establish a 10 x 20 yard grid and a center line. (See Figure 2-4.) Two attackers and one defender are designated within each group. The two attackers stand at diagonal corners of the grid; the defender stands at the center of the grid. One attacking player will have a ball at his feet, and the other will be in a push-up position.

On the coach's command, the supporting attacker must complete one push-up, jump to his feet, and race beyond the center line to lend support in the ball carrier's zone. (This part of the drill helps to instill a sense of urgency in going to the support of a ball carrier.) Meanwhile the defender attempts to tackle the ball away from the ball carrier before the support arrives.

Once the supporting player is in the same zone as the ball carrier, they will dribble and pass the ball in an attempt to place it on the goal line (the regulation touchline).

The players change roles after each goal or, if no goals are scored, after twenty to thirty-five seconds. If the defender wins the ball over, the game is restarted immediately.

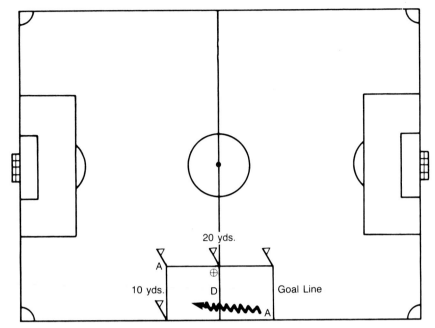

FIGURE 2-4

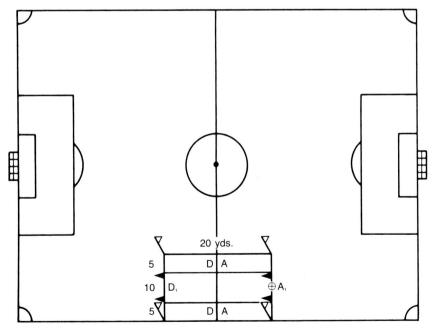

FIGURE 2-5

Players: In groups of six
Ages: Twelve and older
Playing Area: 20 x 20 yard grids
Equipment: One soccer ball and eight markers per group
Time: Nine minutes

For each group of six players, four markers are placed to establish a 20 x 20 yard grid along a touchline. Another two markers are placed at each end of a grid to serve as a goal. (See Figure 2-5.)

Each group of players is divided into three attackers and three defenders. Attacker A1 stands on the regulation touchline with a ball at his feet; the two supporting attackers stand in side zones, which run the length of the grid and are five yards wide. Defender D1 is stationed at the end of the grid opposite A1; the remaining two defenders are positioned in the side zones and are instructed that they may not leave their respective zones at any time.

On the coach's signal, D1 begins to race across the grid to challenge A1. Meanwhile, A1 is dribbling into the center zone, and the supporting attackers are moving within their side zones in an attempt to lose their defenders. Once a supporting attacker is clear, A1 executes a pass (under pressure from D1). If the pass is successful, and if the supporting attacker is then able to dribble into the center zone without losing the ball to his defender, a two versus one situation is created (since the defenders in the side zones are not permitted into the center zone). These two attackers now attempt to bring the third attacker into the center zone in the same fashion, creating a three versus one. Once all three attackers are in the center zone, they go for a goal.

If the ball is won over by D1, he will change places with the attacker who lost the ball, and the game is restarted. The attackers and defenders also change roles whenever a goal is scored.

Variation

If D1 wins the ball over at the outset against A1, he changes roles with A1 and immediately tries to bring in a supporting attacker.

If D1 wins the ball over in a two versus one situation, he may bring in the original supporting defender from the side zone vacated by an attacker. In this case, the supporting attacker must race back to prevent the pass and, if unsuccessful, must remain in the side zone.

If D1 wins the ball over in a three versus one, the two supporting attackers must return to their respective side zones before their opponents can be brought into the center zone.

Players: In groups of six
Ages: Twelve and older
Playing Area: 15 x 20 yard grids

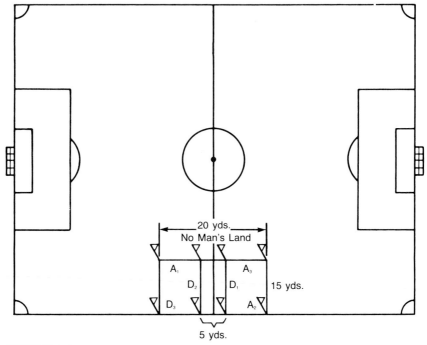

FIGURE 2-6

Equipment: One ball and eight markers per group
Time: Nine minutes

Four markers are placed to establish each 15 x 20 yard grid. Two additional markers are placed five yards apart at each side of a grid to delineate a "no man's land." (See Figure 2-6.) A group of six players, three attackers and three defenders, is assigned to each grid, with either attacker A2 or A3 in possession of a ball.

On the coach's command, A2 and A3 play keep-away (passing and dribbling) from defender D1 while remaining on their own side of no man's land. Meanwhile, A1 moves in such a way as to lose defenders D2 and D3, in an attempt to receive and return a pass to A2 or A3, whoever is clear of D1 at the time. Once A2 or A3 has successfully received the return pass from A1, he may dribble and pass his way across no man's land to join A1 and create a two versus two situation. These two attackers will then attempt to bring the remaining attacker across no man's land in the same fashion, thus creating a three versus two. Once in a three versus two, the attackers attempt to complete five consecutive passes, at which point the game is restarted.

If D1 wins the ball over from A2 or A3 at the outset, his team becomes the attackers and the game continues in the same manner.

Variation

A goalkeeper is added and positioned in no man's land. The goalie attempts to intercept passes through that area, in which case the ball passes over to the defending team and the game restarts.

Players: In groups of six
Ages: Twelve and older
Playing Area: 15 x 15 yard grid at center of field
Equipment: One ball and four markers
Time: Nine minutes

Four markers are placed to establish a 15 x 15 yard grid at the very center of the field. The players are divided into groups of six, three attackers and three defenders. As each group takes its turn participating in the exercise, one attacker and one defender will be stationed at a corner of the grid; another pair stand at the diagonally opposite corner; and the third pair, attacker A1 and defender D1, are positioned at the center of the grid. (See Figure 2-7.) Attacker A1 will have a soccer ball at his feet.

On the coach's command, A1 will play keep-away from defender D1 until such time that a supporting attacker, A2 or A3, is free of his defender. A2 and A3

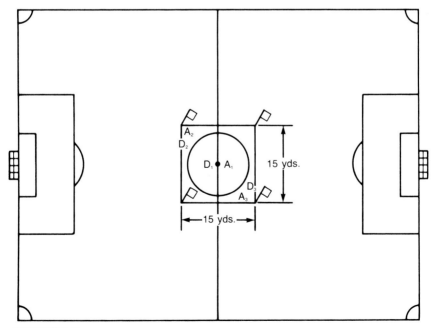

FIGURE 2-7

may move anywhere within the grid except the center circle. Once a supporting attacker is free, A1 will pass the ball to bring that attacker into the center circle, creating a two versus one situation. These two attackers will now play keep-away until such time that the remaining attacker is free of his defender. Once clear, the remaining attacker is brought into the center circle in the same fashion, creating a three versus one. Once in a three versus one, the attackers attempt to complete five consecutive passes, at which point all the players assume their original positions and the next round of play begins.

If D1 wins the ball over at the outset against A1, his team becomes the attackers and the game continues in the same manner. If D2 or D3 intercepts a pass, he passes the ball to D1 and his team becomes the attackers.

Variation

Upon controlling a pass from a player in the center circle (either as an attacker or a defender), a supporting player will attempt to maintain possession until the other supporting attacker or defender is clear to receive a pass through or around the center circle. This receiving player then attempts to pass the ball back to his teammate in the center circle, following the pass to create a two versus one. The teammate remaining outside the circle is brought in as in the original exercise, above.

Players: In one or two groups of seven
Ages: Fourteen and older
Playing Area: Half-field
Equipment: One ball and four markers per group
Time: Fifteen minutes

Four markers are placed to establish a grid of approximately 20 x 30 yards, as in Figure 2-8. The players are divided into groups of seven—four attackers, two defenders, and a goalkeeper. The goalie stands at the center of the goal cage; attacker A1 stands at the penalty spot with a ball in his hands; A2 is at the lower infield corner of the goal area; A3 is in the center circle; A4 stands at the intersection of the center line and the touchline. Defender D1 stands in the retaining arc, and D2 assumes a push-up position in the infield corner of the grid toward the center line.

On the coach's command, A1 full volley kicks (from the hands) the ball to the goalkeeper. Simultaneously, A2 races to the lower left-hand corner of the grid to receive a thown pass from the goalie. A1 races to the top left-hand corner of the grid, and A3 and A4 move to the right-hand corners of the grid.

Defenders D1 and D2 race into the grid to pressure the attackers and attempt to win the ball over. The attackers play keep-away and attempt to complete five consecutive passes. Once five passes are completed or the ball is intercepted, the game is restarted and the players rotate positions.

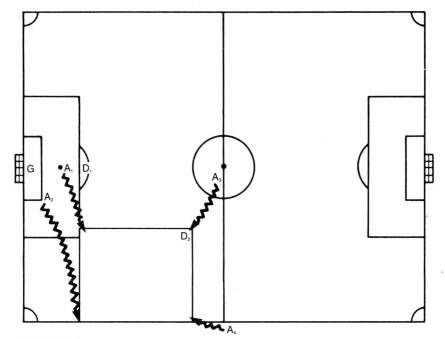

FIGURE 2-8

Variation 1

The goalkeeper throws a pass to A3, who controls the ball and brings it quickly into the grid. Defender D2 has been positioned in the corner diagonally across from his original position; that is, D2 has lined up initially at the lower right-hand corner of the grid.

Variation 2

The goalkeeper passes to A4. In this case, D1 has lined up with A3 in the center circle.

Players: One or two groups of twelve
Ages: Fourteen and older
Playing Area: Half-field
Equipment: One ball and six markers per group
Time: Thirty minutes

Markers are placed in such a way as to divide half the field into three equal zones, with the width of each zone equal to the width of the penalty area (eighteen

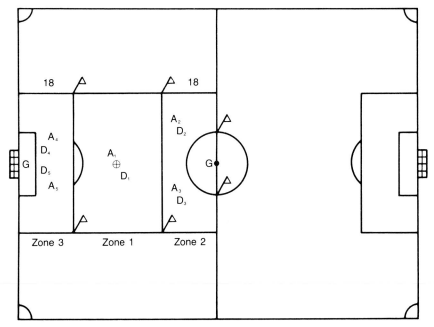

FIGURE 2-9

yards). The regulation goal cage serves as one goal; markers placed on the center line constitute the other goal.

Twelve players are divided into two teams of five fielders and one goalkeeper. The players assume the positions indicated in Figure 2-9.

The game begins when the coach drops the ball between the two players in Zone 1. The player winning the ball (A1, in the figure) attempts to maintain possession within Zone 1 until such time that a supporting *back* player (A2 or A3) is free of defenders D2 and D3. Once clear, A1 passes the ball to the supporting back player, who may either pass the ball back to A1 and follow the pass into the center zone, or may dribble the ball into the center zone. The defenders may not enter the center zone; thus a two versus one situation is created.

The two attackers in the center zone now play keep-away from D1 until the remaining back attacker is free for a pass, so that he, too, may be brought into the center zone in like manner, creating a three versus one. If this is accomplished, the three attackers now play keep-away from D1 until a forward supporting attacker (A4 or A5) is free of D4 and D5. Once clear, a pass is made to the free attacker, who will play the ball back to any of the three attackers who is clear in the center zone. If the pass is successful, the receiving attacker in the center zone may enter Zone 3, joining A4 and A5 and going for goal.

Supporting back players (in this case, A2 and A3) must always be brought into the center zone first. Whenever a goal is scored, the players rotate positions. If the defenders win the ball over, in any of the zones, the ball is passed quickly to D1 and the defenders become the attackers.

Variation

A goalkeeper punts or throws the ball into the center zone to start the game.

PENETRATION IN ATTACK

Penetration in attack means creating situations that allow the ball carrier or a supporting attacker to dribble or pass the ball between defenders, thus taking the defenders out of the play. Since, conceivably, as many as ten defenders can be eliminated from a play taking place near the goal, penetration can prove to be a devastating weapon. Sizing up the situation and moving the ball quickly are necessary, however.

In Figure 2-10, the ball carrier, RM, passes the ball to RW, who is immediately pressured by defender LB. RW lays off a quick pass to CF2, after which RW sprints beyond defender LB (equivalent to "the old give-and-go" in basketball). Player CF2

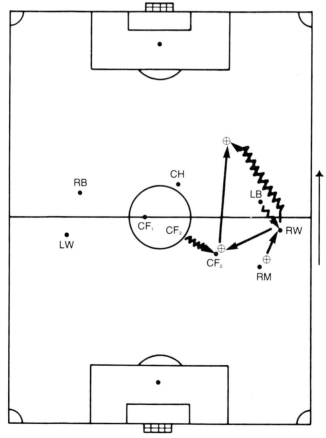

FIGURE 2-10

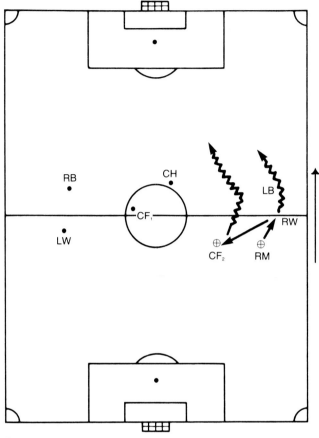

FIGURE 2-11

quickly takes advantage of defenders RB, CH, and LB by executing a *penetrating* pass between CH and LB to player RW.

Figure 2-11 presents the same situation. This time, however, CF2 chooses not to pass the ball, but rather dribbles in the direction of defender LB, who must now be aware of both CF2 as the ball carrier and RW as a potential pass receiver. In this case, CF2 quickly changes direction and *penetrates* the space between defenders CH and LB.

The following drills are designed to help young players recognize situations that can lead to penetration of the defense.

Players: In groups of three
Ages: Twelve and older
Playing Area: One side of field
Equipment: One ball per group
Time: Nine minutes

The players are divided into groups of three, two attackers and one defender. Attacking players A1 stand along a touchline facing infield, each with a ball at his feet and spaced approximately ten yards apart. For each A1, supporting attacker A2 stands some thirty yards infield, facing A1. The defender stands midway between the two attackers, facing A2.

On the coach's command, A1 chips the ball over the defender to A2, who must bring the ball under control quickly and make a return pass to A1. Once the first chip pass has been made, the defender chases A2 in an attempt to prevent the return pass. Once A2 has controlled the ball, A1 may move laterally and forward to create a better passing angle and to penetrate the defense.

Players rotate positions every thirty-five seconds, with each player taking three turns at each of the three positions.

Variation

A1 is positioned at the part of the center circle nearest a goal. A2 stands at the retaining arc. The defender stands midway between the attackers.

A1 again chips the ball over the defender to A2 and follows his pass. A2 then lays off a first-time pass to A1, and the attackers go for goal. Once A1's pass has passed over his head, the defender attempts to win the ball over.

The coach may or may not wish to insert a goalkeeper for this exercise.

Players: Ten players at a time
Ages: Twelve and older
Playing Area: Between penalty areas
Equipment: Two soccer balls and eight markers
Time: Twelve minutes

Markers are placed to establish two grids of 12 x 12 yards to the sides of the center circle (toward the goals). The two grids should be approximately twenty yards apart. (See Figure 2-12 on page 36.)

Ten players are positioned as follows: four attackers at the corners of Grid 1 and two defenders within Grid 1; four attackers at the corners of Grid 2. One attacker, A1, will have a ball at his feet.

On the coach's command, A1 passes in any direction to a supporting attacker within his grid and these four attackers play keep-away from the two defenders. The attackers try to create a situation in which either A3 or A4 (the attackers nearer the center circle) can make a penetrating ground pass between the defenders. As soon as this is accomplished, the receiving attacker (A1 or A2) makes a lofted pass into Grid 2 and both A1 and A2 follow the pass. The last man to reach Grid 2 takes five push-ups.

The players in Grid 2, meanwhile, have been passing a spare ball, practicing technique. The moment the ball arrives from Grid 1, the spare ball is played across to Grid 1. Players A1 and A2 now become the defenders in Grid 2, and the game continues as before. (Grid 1 players now use the spare ball to practice technique.)

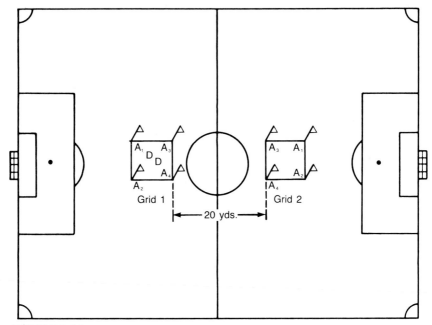

FIGURE 2-12

The players rotate positions intermittently, with A3 and A4 replacing A1 and A2, the defenders replacing A3 and A4, and A1 and A2 replacing the defenders. This rotation system applies to both grids. Note: In each grid, the players standing nearer the goals will always be players A1 and A2, i.e., the players who follow a lofted pass into the other grid.

Variation

Two target men and two additional defenders are introduced into the exercise. A target man is stationed at each retaining arc. An additional defender stands at each goal.

A3 or A4 again makes a penetrating pass before A1 or A2 can loft a pass to Grid 2. Once the lofted pass is made, the attackers in Grid 2 must complete five consecutive passes (under pressure from A1 and A2, once they arrive) before they can pass the ball to the target man at their end of the field. In this case, the target man controls the ball and the added defender moves out from the goal to mark the target man and prevent a shot on the goal.

When a goal is scored or the additional defender wins the ball over, the game is restarted in the grid. The coach may wish to require a greater or fewer number of passes to be completed within a grid before the pass to the target man, depending upon the ability of the players.

Players: In two groups of five
Ages: Twelve and older
Playing Area: Half-field for each group
Equipment: One soccer ball per group
Time: Ten minutes

Two groups of five players are each divided into three attackers, one defender, and one goalkeeper. For each group, attacker A1 has a soccer ball and is positioned to one side of the center circle and just inside the center line. (See Figure 2-13.) Attacker A2 and the defender stand at the retaining arc. A3 is stationed across the field from A1, to the other side of the center circle. The goalkeeper assumes his usual position.

On the coach's command, A1 kicks a lofted or ground pass diagonally across the field for A2, who is marked tightly by the defender. The moment the ball has been passed, A1 begins to jog downfield, as indicated in Figure 2-13, and A3 moves quickly to receive a first-time back pass from A2. The moment A3 reaches the ball, he immediately makes a lead pass for A1, who moves onto the ball at speed and shoots on goal. The defender is free to pressure A1 when he sees the lead pass being made.

The players rotate positions within their half of the field.

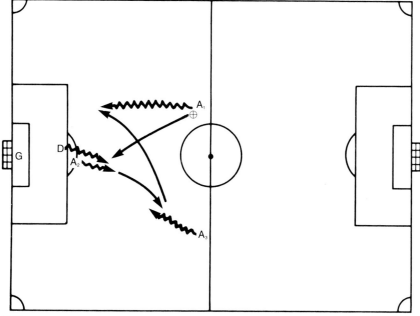

FIGURE 2-13

Variation

A second defender is introduced into the game and lines up on the goal side of the center circle. This defender moves to challenge A3 the moment the ball is played back from A2. If A1 is not open for a shot on goal after receiving the lead pass from A3, the three attackers continue play in a three versus two situation and go for goal.

Players: One or two groups of nine
Ages: Twelve and older
Playing Area: Half-field for one group
Equipment: One ball and four markers per group
Time: Fifteen minutes

Four markers are placed to establish a 12 x 15 yard grid outside the penalty area, with the twelve yard sides parallel to the top of the penalty area. (See Figure 2-14.)

A group of nine players is assigned to a grid and is divided into five attackers, three defenders, and one goalkeeper. Attackers A1 and A2 stand at the corners of the grid toward the center circle; A3 and A4 are positioned at the corners toward the goal; A5 stands in the retaining arc. Defenders D1 and D2 are stationed within

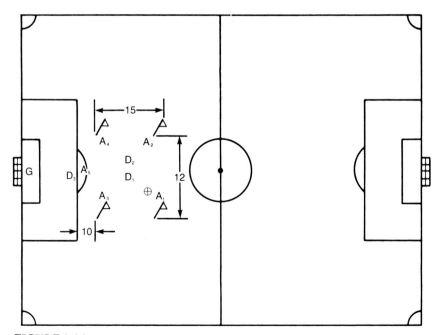

FIGURE 2-14

the grid, and D3 stands at the retaining arc. The goalkeeper assumes his usual position. Attacker A1 has a ball at his feet.

On the coach's command, A1 begins play by passing the ball to any supporting attacker except A5. A1, A2, A3, and A4 then play keep-away from D1 and D2, who exert heavy pressure. The ball is played around the grid until such time that either A1 or A2 can make a penetrating pass between the defenders to A5, who has remained within the retaining arc. A1, A2, and the two defenders follow the pass to create a three versus three situation. A5 may move anywhere within the retaining arc (under passive pressure from D3) before laying off a first-time pass, or controlling and passing to A1 or A2, one of whom will take a first-time shot on goal.

After each shot on goal, the players rotate positions: A1 and A2 become A5 and D3; A5 and D3 become D1 and D2; D1 and D2 become A3 and A4; A3 and A4 become A1 and A2.

Variation

Two target men, A6 and A7, are stationed within ten-yard square grids to the outside top corners of the penalty area. An additional defender, D4, is positioned to one side of the goal area. (See Figure 2-15.)

The four attackers in the original grid may now attempt a penetrating pass to any target man (A5, A6, or A7). If the pass is successful, for example to A7, the

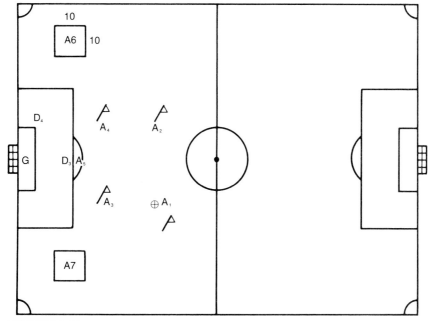

FIGURE 2-15

other two target men (A5 and A6) may leave their zones, as may defenders D3 and D4, creating a three versus two as the attackers go for goal.

When a goal is scored or an interception made, the game is restarted in the original grid. Additional defenders may be added at the coach's discretion.

Players: Any number
Ages: Twelve and older
Playing Area: Full field
Equipment: One soccer ball
Time: Fifteen minutes

Two attackers, A1 and A2, and two defenders, D1 and D2, are positioned at the center circle as in Figure 2-16. A goalkeeper is assigned to each end of the field. The remainder of the players are divided as equally as possible into two groups of supporting attackers, A3's and A4's, and are positioned as in Figure 2-16.

On the coach's command, goalkeeper G1 punts the ball in the direction of A1, who moves quickly to control the ball under pressure from D1. Once the ball is under control, the first player in the line of supporting attackers A3 moves quickly to receive a back pass from A1. When he receives the ball, A3 immediately passes it into the opponents' half of the field. A2 races onto the pass under pressure from D2.

Depending upon the situation, A2 may immediately go for goal or may wait for A1 and A3 to create a three versus two situation, in which case all three attackers go for goal.

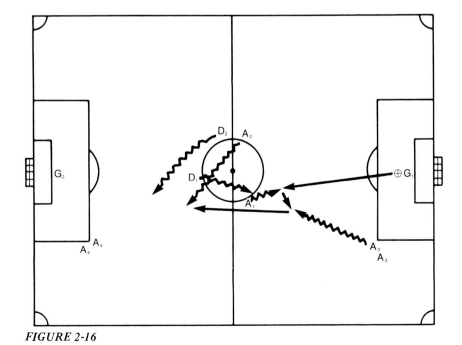

FIGURE 2-16

When a shot is taken on G2, or when the defenders win the ball over, the attackers and defenders return to their original positions, except that A3 lines up at the opposite penalty area, behind the A4's. (The coach may wish to have all players rotate positions instead.) Goalkeeper G2 then restarts the game, which progresses in the opposite direction.

Players: In groups of five
Ages: Twelve and older
Playing Area: Anywhere on field
Equipment: One ball and nine markers per group
Time: Twelve minutes

Four markers are placed to establish a 15 x 20 yard grid for each group of five players. Two sets of markers are also placed, each set one yard apart, to establish goals as in Figure 2-17, and a flag is positioned at the center of one twenty-yard end of the grid.

For each grid, the five players are divided into three attackers and two defenders and are positioned as in Figure 2-17. Attacker A1 will have a ball at his feet.

On the coach's command, the attackers play keep-away from the defenders. The attackers may pass and move anywhere within the grid in an attempt to draw the defenders away from the goals, so a supporting attacker can receive a pass through a goal. Such a penetrating pass will count as one score. A penetrating pass between the defenders that is received by a supporting attacker at the flag (the sup-

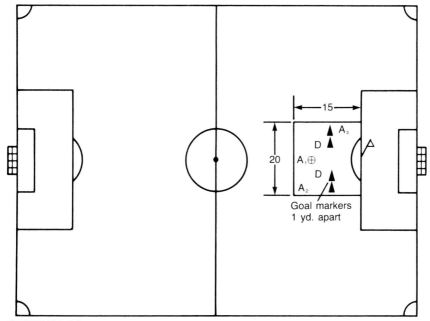

FIGURE 2-17

porting attacker must be facing the ball carrier at the time) will count as two scores.

If a defender wins the ball over, he will replace the attacker who lost the ball.

Variation 1

If the defenders win the ball over, they will replace two of the attackers. A1 is designated to remain an attacker at all times, ensuring a continuous three versus two situation.

Variation 2

An attacking player who receives a penetrating pass at the flag may turn and shoot on the regulation field goal. The coach may or may not wish to add a goal-keeper for this variation.

Players: In groups of six
Ages: Fourteen and older
Playing Area: Anywhere on field
Equipment: One ball and four markers per group
Time: Twenty minutes

Four markers are placed to establish a 15 x 30 yard grid for each group of six players (four attackers and two defenders). For each group, the attackers are positioned at the corners of the grid, one with a soccer ball at his feet, and the defenders stand within the grid.

On the coach's command, the attackers proceed to chip or ground-pass the ball over or between the defenders, attempting to complete five consecutive passes. The defenders exert heavy pressure in an effort to win the ball over and may use their hands to intercept.

If the attackers complete a penetrating ground pass between the defenders, the defenders must take one lap around the grid and will remain as defenders for the next round of play. If the defenders intercept, all attackers must take five push-ups and the players rotate positions. The players also rotate positions whenever the attackers complete five passes.

Variation 1

A 15 x 30 yard grid is established to each side of the center circle and on the goal side of the center line. Two target men (strikers) and a goalkeeper are introduced to the exercise. The target men are stationed at the top corners of the penalty area, directly in line with their respective grids. (See Figure 2-18.)

The four attackers in each grid attempt a penetrating pass to their corresponding target man while under pressure from the defenders. If the pass is successful, the target man controls the ball and shoots on goal.

The players rotate positions after each shot on goal.

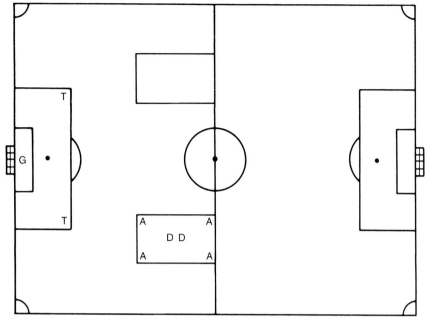

FIGURE 2-18

Variation 2

In addition to the target men and goalkeeper in Variation 1, two additional defenders are also introduced, one stationed at each goalpost. When a penetrating pass to a target man is successful, the defender at the nearer goalpost races out to mark the target man and prevent a shot on goal.

The players rotate positions after each shot on goal or interception.

Variation 3

The same as Variation 2, except that the attacker who completes the penetrating pass may follow the ball and support the target man, going for goal in a two versus one situation against the defender.

The players rotate positions after each shot on goal or interception.

Note: The coach may wish to experiment with the many combinations suitable to this drill, for example, refining Variation 3 by allowing a defender within the grid to follow the attacker's pass, thus creating a two versus two when the attackers go for goal, or allowing two attackers and two defenders to follow the pass, etc.

Players: Fourteen players
Ages: Fourteen and older

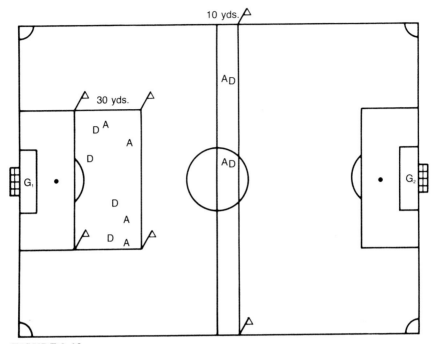

FIGURE 2-19

Playing Area: Full field
Equipment: One soccer ball and six markers
Time: Fifteen minutes

Markers are placed to establish two grids: a 30 x 44 yard grid extending from one penalty area toward the center line, and a grid ten yards wide, extending across the field and from the center line away from the large grid. (See Figure 2-19.)

Two teams of four are positioned in the large grid, and two teams of two in the small grid. A goalkeeper is assigned to each end of the field.

On the coach's signal, goalkeeper G1 starts play by punting the ball into the large grid. The team gaining possession will play keep-away from their opponents, while the supporting attackers in the small grid attempt to break free of their defenders by hard and intelligent running. Once either supporting attacker is clear, the ball carrier will pass the ball to him, thus bringing him into the large grid and creating a five versus four situation. These five attackers then go for goal against G1.

The game is restarted after each shot on goal. If the defending team wins the ball over while in a four versus four, they become the attackers and attempt to create their own five versus four. If the defenders win the ball over while in a five versus four, the defender who intercepts will attempt and follow a penetrating pass to a supporting player who is free in the small grid. This will create a two versus one, and these two players will go for goal against G2. The original player who left the small grid to create the five versus four will race back to even the sides at two versus two.

The game will always be restarted by G1.

Variation

One team of four and one team of three are assigned to the large grid; two teams of two occupy the small grid. All players are restricted to their respective grids at the outset.

G1 starts play by punting the ball into the large grid. If the four-man team gains possession, they will play keep-away from their three opponents until a supporting teammate in the small grid is free of his defender. Once clear, the ball carrier will pass to this player, who will make a return pass to any of his four teammates in the large grid. This receiver must now play a penetrating pass to either supporting attacker in the small grid, who will be breaking to receive the ball in full stride. (Law 11, Offside, applies.) The passer may follow the ball to create a three versus two. These three players then go for goal against G2. After a shot on goal or an interception, the game is restarted by G1.

If the three-man team wins the ball over at the outset, they will attempt to bring in their supporting players by making successful passes, thus creating a four versus four and then a five versus four, at which point they would go for goal against G1. Once they take a shot on goal or lose the ball, the game is restarted by G1.

WIDTH IN ATTACK

Penetration of the defense, with a run or a pass, involves the principle of width in attack. Wing play is needed to spread out the defenders, and young players must learn to pass, dribble, and seek the ball in the wing areas until the defenders commit themselves. Once this is accomplished, penetrating runs and passes must be quick and decisive.

In Figure 2-20, RM has possession of the ball. RM's supporting players RW and CF are under pressure from defenders LB and CH, with defender RB providing defensive depth. Thus RM decides to pass to teammate LW, who has maintained width at the far touchline. Defender RB must now decide whether to concede the space in front of LW or to close down the space and pressure LW. In closing down the space, RB runs the risks inherent in eliminating the defensive depth he has been providing to LB and CH.

The following drills are designed to accustom young players to the discipline involved in maintaining width in attack.

Players: Up to three groups of five
Ages: Twelve and older
Playing Area: Center circle and similar areas

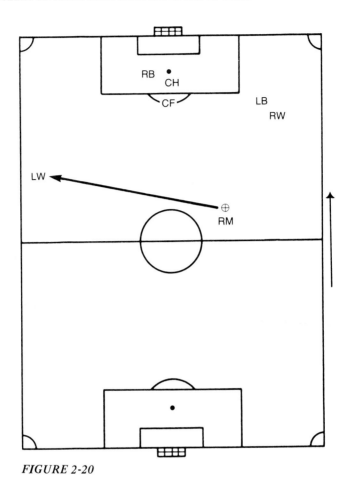

FIGURE 2-20

Equipment: One ball and eight markers per group
Time: Nine minutes

    Up to three circular practice grids are utilized, one being the center circle. The other two grids are formed by extending the curve of the retaining arcs through the penalty areas and into the goal areas. (See Figure 2-21.) For each circle, four goals, consisting of markers placed one yard apart, are established as in Figure 2-21.

    Five players are assigned to each grid, two defenders and three attackers (including a "designated attacker," who will remain on the ball side at all times). Each team will have three goals to defend and, when in possession of the ball, three goals to attack.

    The game begins with the three-man attacking team in possession of the ball. On the coach's signal, the three-man team attacks goals G1, G2, and G3 by playing keep-away and attempting to draw the defenders away from these goals with intel-

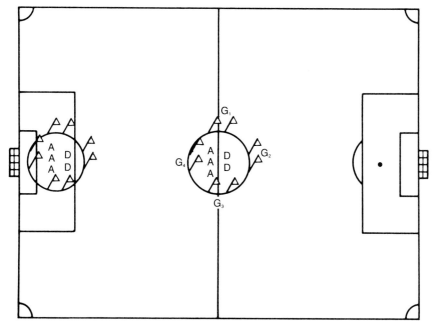

FIGURE 2-21

ligent running on and off the ball. A goal is scored by dribbling through a set of markers, after which the game is restarted.

If the defenders win the ball over, they immediately team up with the designated attacker and go for their opponents' goals (G3, G4, and G1).

Variation

One of the original defenders (from the two-man team) will be a goalkeeper and may use his hands while on defense.

Players: One group of thirteen
Ages: Fourteen and older
Playing Area: Center field
Equipment: One soccer ball and eighteen markers
Time: Thirty minutes

Markers are placed to establish four goals at the corners of a 30 x 40 yard grid at the center of the field. Four additional pairs of markers are placed to serve as goals on the center circle. One marker is placed at the midpoint of the sides of the grid that are parallel to the center line. (See Figure 2-22.)

The players are divided into two teams of six, with a thirteenth player chosen to be the "designated attacker," who will remain on the offense at all times. Two

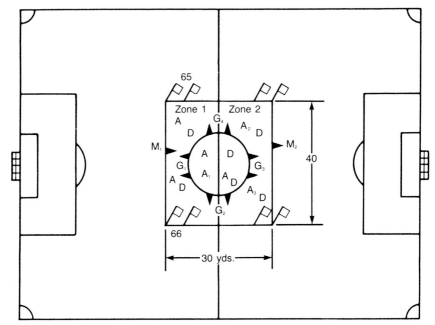

FIGURE 2-22

players from each team assume positions in the center circle; another two from each team stand outside the circle to either side of the center line.

The coach starts the game by throwing the ball into the center circle. The team that wins the ball will have the advantage of an extra player (the designated attacker), thus creating a three versus two situation. The team with the ball (the A's in Figure 2-22) will play keep-away from their opponents and, with intelligent movement on and off the ball, will attempt to set up the designated attacker such that he can score by dribbling through any one of three goals—G1, G2, or G3. Once this has been accomplished, the designated attacker will join the two attackers in Zone 1, outside the center circle, thus creating another three versus two. Any one of these three may score by dribbling the ball through Goal 5 or Goal 6 at the corners of the grid, or by striking the single marker M1 with the ball, under pressure from the two defenders in Zone 1.

If the ball is won over by the defenders at the outset (in the center circle), the designated attacker will switch teams and join in an attack on G1, G3, or G4. The game then continues as before, but with the other team on the attack.

If the ball is won over outside the center circle, the ball must be played to the designated attacker, who will dribble back to the center circle under pressure from the players who lost the ball. The designated attacker will then team up with the new attackers for a continuation of the game.

Goals scored by dribbling between markers on the center circle count as single goals. Goals scored outside the center circle count one and cause the game to be restarted in the center circle. Any goal scored by striking a single marker counts double.

The designated attacker is the only player permitted to pass between the center circle and the outer grid. The designated attacker should be replaced at approximately five-minute intervals.

Variation

Target men may be introduced and stationed within the retaining arcs. Once a goal is scored by dribbling through the markers at the corners of the grid, the ball is passed to the appropriate (nearer) target man for a shot on the regulation field goal. Additional defenders may also be introduced to mark the target men, at the coach's discretion.

Players: One or two groups of eight
Ages: Fourteen and older
Playing Area: Half of field per group
Equipment: One ball and two markers per group

Two markers are placed eight yards apart just to the goal side of the center line to serve as one goal for a half-field game. Eight players are divided into two teams of three plus two goalkeepers. One player from each team is positioned in a

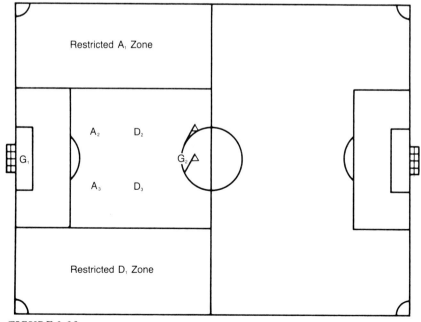

FIGURE 2-23

restricted zone, extending along the touchline and from the touchline to the penalty area. (See Figure 2-23.) The goalkeepers assume their usual positions; all other players stand in the free zone (the portion of the field between the restricted zones).

On the coach's signal, goalkeeper G1 starts play by distributing the ball to the attacker in a wide position (player A1, who is confined to the restricted zone). Once A1 has received the ball, a defender in the free zone (D2 or D3) must commit himself, applying pressure to A1. Player A1 now passes the ball to A2 or A3, creating a two versus one situation in the free zone. These two attackers go for goal, attempting a shot on G2 before the absent defender can recover to create a two versus two. Once the shot has been taken, G2 restarts the game by distributing the ball to D1 and the game continues in the same fashion, but with the original defenders now on the attack.

At any time the ball is won over the defenders, the ball is passed back to their goalkeeper, who restarts the game.

Variation

D1 is stationed at a top corner of the penalty area and starts play by centering the ball into the goal area for G1 to gather. At this moment, A1 races from his marker (positioned as in Figure 2-24) to receive the ball from G1 in the free zone.

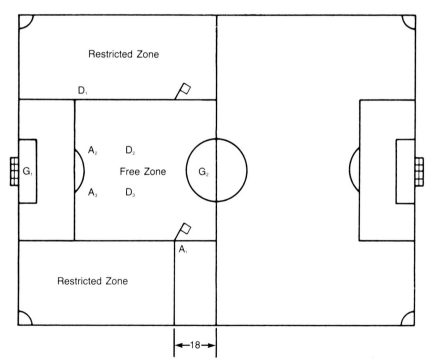

FIGURE 2-24

The exercise now continues as a three versus two in the free zone; otherwise, the rules are the same as in the original exercise. Players D1 and A1 always start the game, and the players change roles at the coach's discretion.

Players: One or two groups of fifteen
Ages: Fourteen and older
Playing Area: Half-field per group
Equipment: One ball and two markers per group
Time: Twenty-five minutes

Two markers are placed eight yards apart just to the goal side of the center line to serve as one goal for a half-field game. Fifteen players are divided into two teams of six, plus two goalkeepers and a "designated attacker," who will play on the offense at all times. A pair of players, one from each team, is stationed in each of two restricted zones, which run along the touchlines and extend from the touchlines to the penalty area. (See Figure 2-25.) The designated attacker and two players from each team are stationed in the free zone, which is the portion of the field between the restricted zones. Target men stand outside the ends of each restricted zone. The goalkeepers assume their usual positions.

On the coach's signal, goalkeeper G1 starts play by punting the ball into the free zone. The team gaining possession of the ball will have the advantage of an extra player (the designated attacker), creating a three versus two situation in the

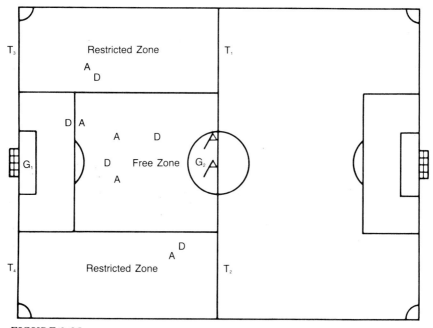

FIGURE 2-25

free zone. This team (the A's in Figure 2-25) will play keep-away from their opponents until such time that the designated attacker is clear to pass the ball to a teammate stationed as a target man (T1 or T2 in the figure). The target man receiving the pass must make a one-touch pass to an attacker in a restricted zone (A1 or A2, whichever has managed to break free of his opponent).

After receiving the pass, A1 or A2 may either dribble the ball into the free zone (the defender remains in the restricted zone) to create a four versus two and go immediately for goal, or if a go-for-goal situation does not exist at the moment, may make a first-time pass to any open attacker in the free zone. In the latter case, the receiving player must make a first-time pass to A1 or A2 to bring the additional attacker into the free zone for a four versus two.

If the defenders win the ball over at the outset in the free zone, the designated attacker will join that team and the game continues as above, except with target men T3 and T4 involved. If a defender in a restricted zone intercepts, he must pass the ball to a teammate in the free zone and the game continues with the ball in that team's possession.

After each shot on goal, the game is restarted by the goalkeeper on whom the shot was taken. Players rotate positions every five minutes, with the designated attacker replacing a player in the free zone and the target men replacing players in the restricted zones.

Players: One group of thirteen
Ages: Fourteen and older
Playing Area: Full field
Equipment: One soccer ball and eight markers
Time: Twenty minutes

Four pairs of markers are placed five yards apart to establish intermediate goals positioned as in Figure 2-26. Thirteen players are divided into two teams of five, plus two goalkeepers and a "designated attacker," who will remain on the offense at all times and who is restricted to the center circle at the outset.

On the coach's signal, one of the goalkeepers starts play by punting the ball into the field of play. The team gaining possession will play keep-away from their opponents until such time that a pass can be played into the designated attacker, who will then dribble the ball out of the center circle to create a six versus five situation as the attackers go for goal (in this example, goal G1). Once out of the center circle, the designated attacker is restricted to two-touch soccer (control and pass) and, whenever receiving the ball from a teammate, his next pass must be *away from the goal being attacked* (G1).

The attackers must dribble or pass the ball through the intermediate goals (B3 and B4) to a supporting attacker beyond before they can go for the regulation goal.

If the defenders win the ball over at the outset of the game, they will team up with the designated attacker and attack intermediate goals B1 and B2 and regulation goal G2. If the defenders intercept while in a six versus five situation, i.e., with

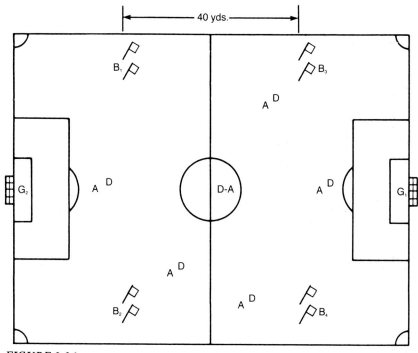

FIGURE 2-26

the designated attacker in the play, they must play keep-away until the designated attacker can race back to the center circle, at which point he may be brought back into the game in the usual fashion.

After each shot on goal, the game is restarted by the goalkeeper on whom the shot was taken.

Players: One or two groups of eight
Ages: Fourteen and older
Playing Area: Half of field per group
Equipment: One ball and eight markers per group
Time: Twenty-five minutes

For each group of eight players, four pairs of markers are placed five yards apart, two pairs near the intersection of the center line and each touchline, two pairs near the top corners of the penalty area. (See Figure 2-27.) The eight players are divided into two teams of three plus two "designated attackers," who will remain on the offense at all times. Goals G1 and G2 are assigned to one team, goals G3 and G4 to the other.

Play starts when the coach punts the ball into the field of play. The team gaining possession will have the advantage of two extra players (the designated

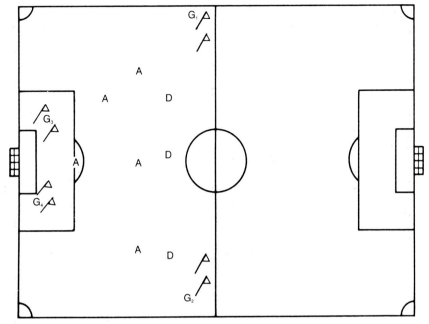

FIGURE 2-27

attackers). In Figure 2-27, the A's have possession of the ball and are attempting to score on goal G1. Whenever a designated attacker receives the ball, however, he must either make a strong run (while dribbling) or immediately pass in the direction of the other goal (in this case, G2).

Whenever a goal is scored, the designated attackers join the opposite team in attacking the goals at the other end of the field. If the defenders win the ball over, they must play keep-away until the designated attackers can move behind them before an attack on goal can proceed.

Variation

The designated attackers are restricted to two-touch soccer (control and pass). Whenever a designated attacker receives the ball, he must pass to the other designated attacker, who may dribble to either goal or may pass the ball to a supporting attacker for a shot on goal.

Players: One group of twenty
Ages: Fourteen and older
Playing Area: Full field
Equipment: Two soccer balls and eight markers
Time: Fifteen minutes

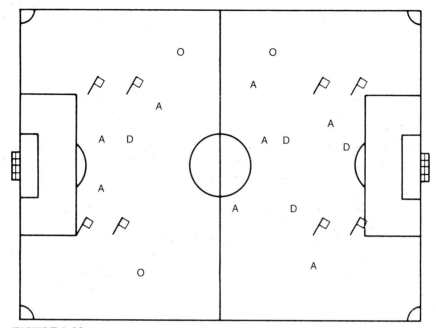

FIGURE 2-28

Pairs of markers are placed eight yards apart to establish four goals just in-field from the top corners of each penalty area. (See Figure 2-28.) Twenty players are divided into two teams of eight plus two goalkeepers per team and are positioned as in the figure.

Play begins when the coach kicks two balls into the field of play. The team or teams gaining possession (one team may gain possession of both balls) will then attack the goals located at their opponents' end of the field.

Goals are scored either by dribbling past the goalkeeper and between the markers (in either direction), or by passing the ball past the goalkeeper to a supporting player behind the goal (in either direction).

If the ball passes out of play over a touchline, the opposing team restarts play with a throw-in. When a team scores at any of the four goals, the game is restarted by the coach. If a goalkeeper makes a save, he distributes the ball to his teammates.

The coach may wish to conduct the exercise with only one ball to avoid confusion. Special emphasis should be placed on Law 12, governing fouls and misconduct.

Players: One group of twelve
Ages: Fourteen and older
Playing Area: Center field
Equipment: One ball and eight markers
Time: Twenty minutes

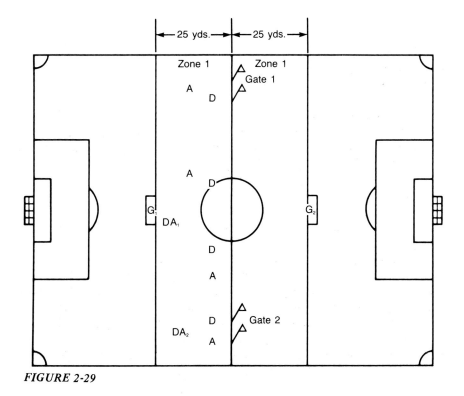

FIGURE 2-29

Two goals are established with markers placed eight yards apart and twenty-five yards to either side of the center line. Two gates, consisting of markers placed six yards apart, are set up on the center line, midway between the center spot and each touchline. (See Figure 2-29.) Twelve players are divided into two teams of four, plus two goalkeepers and two "designated attackers" (who will remain on offense at all times).

The game begins in Zone 1, with the players positioned as in Figure 2-29. The designated attackers will play as midfielders in support of the regular attackers. The defenders must protect goal G2, as well as both gates.

To begin play, goalkeeper G1 distributes the ball to either designated attacker. The designated attackers may touch the ball an unlimited number of times, whereas the regular attackers must play two-touch soccer (control and pass). Play continues in Zone 1 until such time that either designated attacker (midfielder) can dribble the ball through a gate, or until a regular attacker can pass the ball through a gate to another attacker in Zone 2. Once the ball is in Zone 2, all players may move into that zone and the attackers go for goal against G2.

If the defenders win the ball over at the outset (in Zone 1), they immediately retreat to Zone 2 and play keep-away until the designated attackers are behind them, ready to support them as they go for goal G1, again by way of a gate.

After each shot on goal, the game is restarted by the goalkeeper against whom the shot was taken, with the attackers and defenders changing roles.

MOBILITY IN ATTACK

Mobility in attack means that the attacking players interchange positions, on and off the ball, in an effort to disorganize the defending team. Diagonal runs across and behind the defenders are usually the most effective ways of pulling defending players out of position or catching them blind-sided. Mobility is also the attackers' best countermeasure against the defensive tactics of delay and concentration (covered later in this section).

Conversely, a *lack* of mobility in attack makes the job of the defenders easier. First, a team that attacks in set positions allows the defender to know immediately which attackers he should be covering and where to find them during the course of a match. Secondly, a team that lacks mobility allows the defender to quickly recognize the strengths and weaknesses of individual attackers and to react accordingly.

In Figure 2-30, the ball carrier is supported by attacking players CF1, CF2, LM, and LW. Attacking player CF1 moves into the position of the right winger,

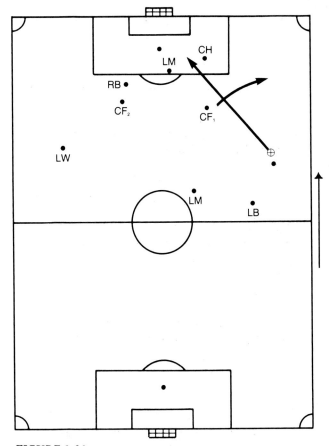

FIGURE 2-30

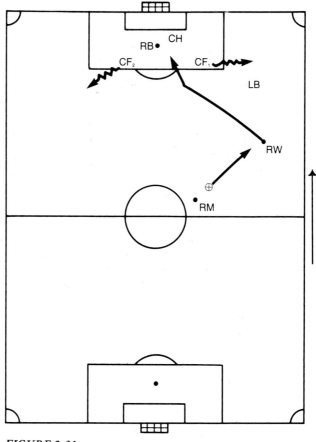

FIGURE 2-31

drawing along defender CH. CF2 holds position and is covered by defenders LM and RB. This leaves an opening in a central position near the top of the penalty area. Attacker LW, seeing this space open up, makes a diagonal run behind defender RB. Defenders RM, LM, and CH are caught watching the ball, concerned with player movement on the ball side. At the right moment, LW calls for a through pass from the ball carrier for a shot on goal.

In Figure 2-31, attacking player RW has received a pass from RM and runs diagonally with the ball, across defender LB and into a central position at the top of the penalty area. At this point, supporting attackers CF1 and CF2 move away, trying to draw away defenders CH and RB. This will free space for RW to shoot, or for a give and go, or, if RW is forced into a passing situation, for a shot by CF1 or CF2.

This subsection does not include drills specifically designed to teach the principle of mobility. Rather, the foregoing discussion is offered in order to present complete coverage of the principles of play. Many drills have already been presented that, while focusing primarily on other principles of attack, have incorporated the basic principle of mobility.

It is hoped that this discussion of mobility will lead the reader to analyze his team's performance in terms of this principle.

ATTACK–GENERAL

The following drills are presented separately because they deal with attack in general and do not focus on any particular principle of attack.

Once the players have become accustomed to application of the principles of depth, penetration, width, and mobility in attack, the coach may wish to conduct the following exercises to reinforce the lessons learned in earlier drills and to illustrate the interrelationship between the various principles of attack.

Players: One group of fifteen
Ages: Twelve and older
Playing Area: Center field
Equipment: Six or more soccer balls and eight markers
Time: Twenty minutes

Eight markers are placed to establish the corners of three contiguous 15 x 15 yard grids. (See Figure 2-32.) A group of five attackers is assigned to each side grid (Zones 1 and 2), and five defenders are assigned to the center grid (the free zone).

The coach starts the game by propelling a ball into Zone 1. The moment one of the players in this zone touches the ball, any two players from the free zone sprint into Zone 1 to try to intercept.

The five attackers in Zone 1 play keep-away until such time that the ball can be played through or over the three remaining players in the free zone and to the five attackers in Zone 2. If this is accomplished, two of the remaining defenders in the free zone rush to Zone 2 to try to intercept, while the two defenders in Zone 1 return to the free zone.

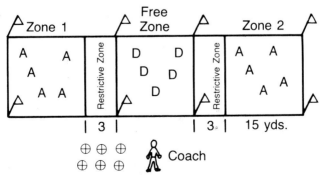

FIGURE 2-32

If the defenders in either grid win the ball over, the ball is passed back to the coach, who restarts the game after the five defenders have changed roles with the five attackers who lost the ball. (Players should be encouraged to move quickly when changing roles.)

Variations

The coach may allow: a) only a given number of passes in Zone 1 before the ball is played to Zone 2; b) lofted passes only; c) two-touch soccer only.

Players: One or two groups of six
Ages: Twelve and older
Playing Area: Half-field per group
Equipment: Six soccer balls and two markers per group
Time: Twenty minutes

For each group, two markers are placed eight yards apart just inside the center line to function as a goal. A goalkeeper is stationed at this goal and at the regulation field goal.

Attacker A1 (a striker) stands midway between the goalkeepers, and A2 (striker) is positioned just to the side of the goal at the center of the field. Two de-

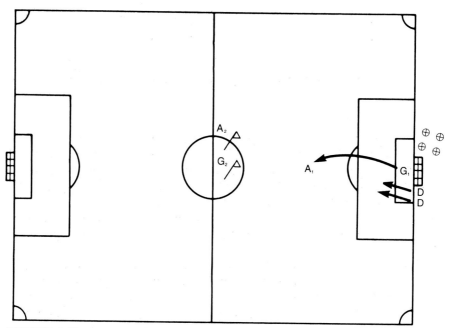

FIGURE 2-33

fenders (sweeper and center back) are positioned to the side of the regulation goal diagonally across from A2. (See Figure 2-33.)

Goalkeeper G1 starts play by distributing the ball, in the air, in the direction of A1. The moment the ball is released, the defenders race out to apply pressure on A1. A1 must now decide whether there is time for a quick shot on goal G2 or whether to bring in A2 and then go for goal.

If the defenders win the ball over, the game is restarted by G2 and the defenders change roles with the attackers.

Variation

An additional attacker, A3, is introduced and stationed at the touchline across the field from A2. G1 again distributes the ball to A1, and the defenders race to apply pressure. A1 may go for goal or bring in A2. A3 may be brought in only after A2 has joined the attack, thus creating a three versus two situation for a shot on goal.

Players: Any number
Ages: Twelve and older
Playing Area: Half-field
Equipment: Six or more soccer balls
Time: Twenty minutes

Two target men, A1 and A2, and two defenders are positioned within, and are restricted to playing within, the retaining arc. The remaining players line up along the center line and are provided with six or more balls.

On the coach's signal, the first player on the center line dribbles the ball at speed toward A1 and A2, who are moving within the retaining arc, and who are man-marked by the defenders. When either A1 or A2 calls for a pass, the ball carrier makes the pass and sprints toward the goal. A1 or A2 must then make a penetrating pass to this sprinting player for a shot on goal, using any number of touches designated by the coach.

A goalkeeper may or may not be included in the exercise.

Variation

When a target man receives a pass, he must play a first-time pass to the supporting target man. If this pass is successful, A1, A2, and the defenders may leave the retaining arc and the attackers go for goal in a three versus two. If the defenders win the ball over, they play the ball back to the next player at the center line.

Players: One or two groups of seven
Ages: Twelve and older
Playing Area: Half-field per group

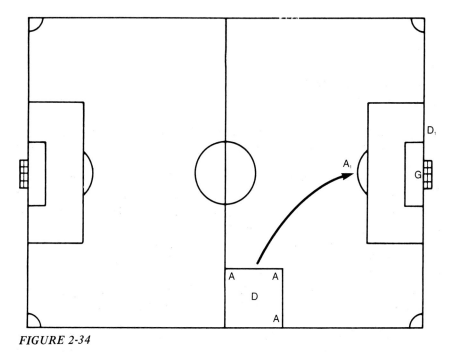

FIGURE 2-34

Equipment: Six soccer balls and four markers per group
Time: Twenty minutes

For each group, markers are placed to establish a 12 x 12 yard grid extending toward the goal from the center line and from a touchline. (See Figure 2-34.) Three attackers and one defender are positioned within the grid. The fourth attacker, A1 (a target man), stands at the retaining arc. The second defender, D1, stands at the goalpost diagonally across from the grid. The goalkeeper assumes his usual position.

The game starts with the three attackers in the grid playing keep-away from the one defender. Depending upon the pressure from the defender, the attackers at any time may pass the ball, along the ground or in the air, to A1, with the passer immediately following the ball. The moment A1 controls the ball, D1 may leave the goalpost to apply pressure on A1. A1 now has two options: to beat the defender and shoot on goal, or to interpass with the supporting player from the grid before going for goal. If D1 wins the ball over, he may pass it back to the grid or to the goalkeeper.

The players rotate positions as follows: D1 replaces the attacker who made the pass; A1 replaces D1 at the goalpost; the passing attacker replaces A1.

Variation

Two additional markers are placed eight yards apart on the center line, next to the grid, to function as a second goal. A second target man, A2, is stationed within the penalty area and is man-marked by an additional defender, D2. Once the pass is made from the grid to either A1 or A2 (the passer again following the ball), D1 races from his goalpost and the three attackers go for goal in a three versus two. If the defenders win the ball over, they assume the attack and go for the second goal on the center line.

The players rotate positions as follows: D1 goes to the grid; D2 goes to the goalpost; A2 replaces D2; the passing attacker replaces A2.

Players: One group of eighteen
Ages: Twelve and older
Playing Area: Full field
Equipment: One soccer ball
Time: Twenty minutes

Eighteen players (eight attackers, six defenders, two target men, and two goal-keepers) are positioned as in Figure 2-35.

On the coach's signal, goalkeeper G1 starts the game by punting the ball into the field of play. Assuming an attacker controls the ball, the attacking team plays two-touch soccer (control and pass) in an attempt to complete a pass to target man T2. T2 will then make a first-time pass (one touch) for a give and go with any supporting attacker who is free of the defense for a shot on G2. G2 will then restart play.

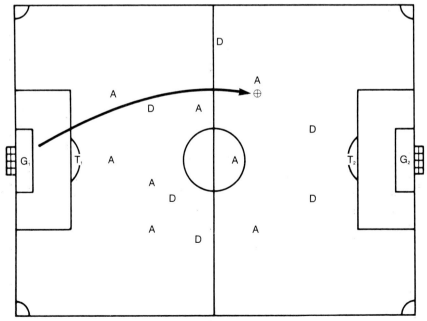

FIGURE 2-35

If the defenders win the ball over at any time, including an opening punt from a goalkeeper, they will play regular soccer (passing, dribbling, etc.) in an attempt to complete a pass to T1. T1 will then make a first-time pass off to any defender who is free for a shot on G1.

Variation

Two additional defenders are introduced to man-mark the target men. Target men follow their passes to create two versus one situations in going for goal.

Players: One or two groups of eight
Ages: Twelve and older
Playing Area: Half-field per group
Equipment: One soccer ball and six markers per group
Time: Nine minutes

For each group of eight players, four markers are placed to establish a grid extending twenty yards from the top of the penalty area toward the center line. Two additional markers are placed eight yards apart just inside the center line to serve as a second goal. (See Figure 2-36.)

The eight players are divided into three attackers, three defenders, and two goalkeepers. Attacker A1 and defender D1 stand just outside the retaining arc;

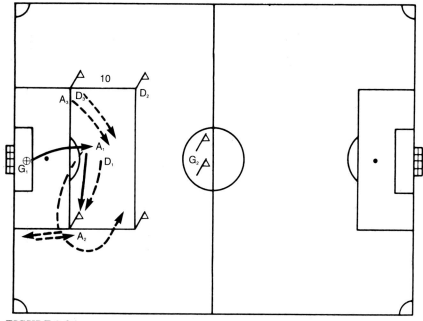

FIGURE 2-36

A2 and D2 stand at corners of the grid diagonally across from one another; A3 and D3 stand at the other end of the penalty area line from A2. The goalkeepers assume the usual positions at the two goals.

Play begins when goalkeeper G1 distributes the ball to A1, who is under passive pressure from D1. A1 controls the ball and passes it to A2, who has just returned to his corner after making a five to ten yard run down the side of the penalty area and back. A2 controls the ball and D1 moves in to apply passive pressure on A2.

A1 now runs to the outside of and around A2, who now has the option of passing to A1 or to A3 (A3 having just broken toward the center of the grid under passive pressure from D3). Once the pass has been executed, D2 may enter the game to create a three versus three situation. The attackers attempt to maintain possession for a shot on goalkeeper G2.

If the defenders win the ball over, they will play it back to G2 and assume their original positions. When play is restarted, however, the defenders will be on the attack against G1.

Whenever a goal is scored, the scoring team will continue on the attack but will now go for the opposite goal.

Players: One group of eleven
Ages: Fourteen and older
Playing Area: Half-field
Equipment: One soccer ball and twelve markers
Time: Thirty minutes

Four markers are placed to establish a 30 x 30 yard grid at the center of the field. Another four markers are placed to represent the corners of a smaller, 15 x 15 yard grid within the larger grid. Four additional markers establish a 10 x 20 yard grid extending from the top of the penalty area toward the center circle. (See Figure 2-37 on page 66.)

Eleven players are divided into five attackers, five defenders, and a goalkeeper. Four attackers and three defenders are stationed within the 15 x 15 yard grid. The fifth attacker (A1 in Figure 2-37) and the fourth defender (D1) stand within the grid near the penalty area. D1 is restricted to passive pressure only. Defender D2 stands at a goalpost, and the goalkeeper assumes his usual position.

On the coach's signal, the four attackers at midfield begin playing keep-away from the three defenders. The attackers must maintain possession of the ball until A1 is clear of D1 (who is offering *passive* pressure) such that A1 can receive a pass. If, before this occurs, the defenders intercept the ball, they will assume the attack and play keep-away from their four opponents, within the larger, 30 x 30 yard grid, until A1 is open for a pass.

Once a pass to A1 has been executed, the passer (either an original attacker or defender) follows his pass to support A1, momentarily creating a two versus one situation against D1. The moment A1 receives the ball, D2 races into the play to support D1 before the two attackers can go for goal.

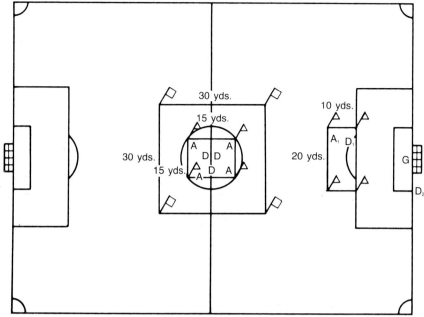

FIGURE 2-37

After a shot on goal, the game is restarted. If D1 and D2 win the ball over before a shot can be taken, they may pass the ball back to the goalkeeper or dribble and pass the ball (under pressure from A1 and A2) back to any one of the original four attackers in the 15 x 15 yard grid.

Players rotate positions at the coach's discretion.

Variation

An additional player, A2, is positioned within the 10 x 20 yard grid, as is D2. An additional defender, D3, assumes D2's former position at the goalpost. Again, the defense (D1 and D2) offers only passive pressure until D3 enters the play.

Players: One or two groups of nine
Ages: Fourteen and older
Playing Area: Half-field
Equipment: One soccer ball and six markers per group
Time: Twenty minutes

For each group, four markers are placed to establish a grid twenty yards wide and extending thirty yards from the top of the penalty area toward the center circle. Two additional markers are placed eight yards apart just inside the center line to function as a second goal. (See Figure 2-38.)

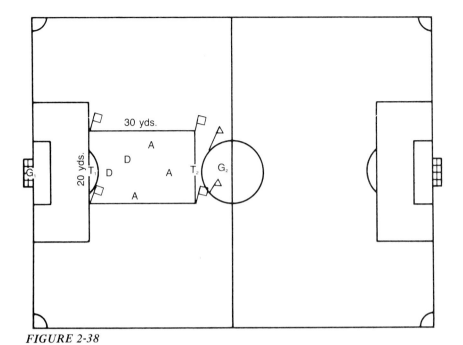

FIGURE 2-38

Three attackers and two defenders are stationed within the grid. Two target men (T1 and T2 in Figure 2-38) stand at the ends of the grid. T1 is restricted to the retaining arc; T2 is permitted to move along the entire end line of the grid. One goalkeeper is assigned to each goal.

On the coach's signal, goalkeeper G2 rolls the ball underhand to any of the three attackers, who will play two-touch soccer (control and pass) until such time that a pass can be made safely to T1. T1 must then lay off a first-time pass (one touch) back to any attacker who is free of the defenders. This receiving attacker will take a shot on goal. After the shot is taken, G1 will restart play and the attackers will play to the opposite goal (G2).

If the defenders win the ball over, they assume the attack and may either dribble or pass the ball to target man T1 or T2, depending upon the direction of play. According to the situation, this target man a) may control the ball until one of the two new attackers (the former defenders) is free for a first-time shot on goal, or b) may make a first-time pass to one of the new attackers for a shot on goal.

Players: One or two groups of eight
Ages: Fourteen and older
Playing Area: Half-field per group
Equipment: Three soccer balls and two markers per group
Time: Twenty minutes

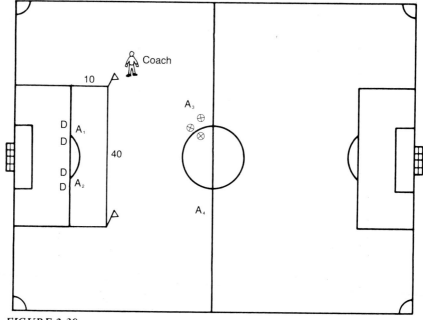

FIGURE 2-39

For each group, two markers are placed to establish two corners of a 10 x 40 yard grid, extending ten yards from the top of the penalty area toward the center circle. (See Figure 2-39.)

Attackers A1 and A2 stand within the grid, at either end of the retaining arc. Attackers A3 and A4 are positioned near the center line, to either side of the center circle. The four defenders are positioned at the top of the penalty area and have the responsibility of marking A1 and A2. (A3 and A4 act as support players only.) Three or more soccer balls are provided to A3.

On the coach's signal, A3 passes a ball along the ground to A1 or A2, who has the following options: a) an immediate shot on goal; b) a combination play with the supporting attacker within the grid and a shot on goal; c) a combination play with the supporting attacker plus the use of A3 and A4 for outlet passes and rebuilding the attack; d) setting up A3 or A4 for a shot on goal (from within the grid area only).

If the defenders win the ball over, the game will be restarted by A3 in the same fashion. Players rotate positions at the coach's discretion.

Players: One or two groups of twelve
Ages: Fourteen and older
Playing Area: Half-field per group
Equipment: Six soccer balls per group
Time: Twenty minutes

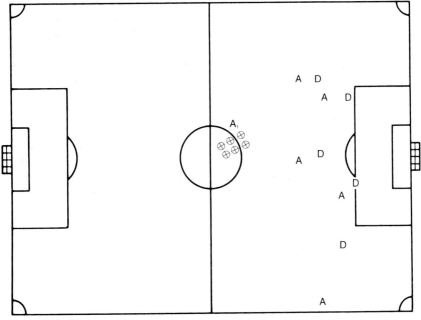

FIGURE 2-40

A group of twelve players (five attackers, five defenders, a playmaker, and a goalkeeper) are positioned within one-half of the field as in Figure 2-40. The playmaker (A1) will start play from near the center circle at all times.

On the coach's signal, the attackers attempt to free themselves of the defenders in order to receive a pass from the playmaker and go for goal. If any ball carrier comes under extreme pressure from a defender, such that he must pass, the ball must be played back to the playmaker, who must then pass to another free attacker. If a defender wins the ball over, he will pass it back to the playmaker and the game will be restarted with the attackers and defenders changing roles.

Variation

A pair of markers is placed four yards apart on the center line, midway between the center spot and each touchline. The playmaker may make a penetrating pass to an attacker for a shot on the regulation field goal, or may make a penetrating run in order to receive a pass for a shot on the regulation goal. If the defenders intercept, they will attempt to score on either of the goals set up on the center line.

Players: All players
Ages: Fourteen and older
Playing Area: Half-field
Equipment: Ten or more soccer balls and twelve markers
Time: Twenty minutes

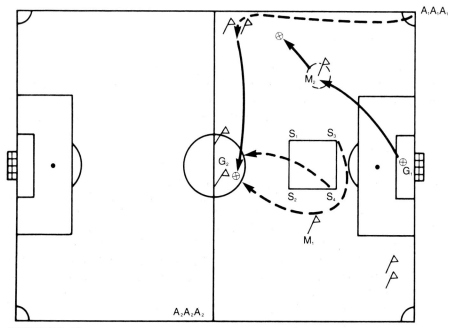

FIGURE 2-41

Four markers are placed to establish a 15 x 15 yard grid just outside the retaining arc. Four strikers (S1, S2, S3, S4) are positioned at the four corners of the grid, and two midfielders (M1, M2) are stationed at markers placed approximately fifteen yards to either side of the grid. (See Figure 2-41.)

Goalkeeper G1 guards the regulation field goal, while G2 mans a goal in the center circle, consisting of two markers placed the usual eight yards apart. Each goalkeeper should have approximately five soccer balls at the ready.

The remainder of the players are divided into two groups of attackers. One group (A1) lines up at a corner flag; the second group (A2) lines up diagonally across the half-field, at the intersection of the center line and the touchline.

A gate, consisting of markers placed one yard apart, is also set up to the left of each goal, some five yards infield of the touchline and five yards infield of the goal line (in one case, the regulation center line).

On the coach's signal, G1 propels a ball to M1, who controls, spins to the outside, and makes as if to dribble downfield toward G2. At the same time, the first player at the corner flag (A1) races downfield, parallel to the touchline, calling for a lead pass from M1. The moment this pass is executed, S3 and S4 begin to *jog*: S3 jogs around S4's marker and toward G2; S4 jogs diagonally across the grid toward S1 and on toward G2.

Meanwhile, A1 continues to dribble at speed toward the gate on his side of the field. A1 dribbles the ball through the gate before making a lofted pass to the front of G2. S3 and S4 then move onto the ball and shoot or head it for the goal.

(At the moment the ball is lofted, S3 and S4 should be moving quickly, not simply standing and waiting for the ball. S4 should be just inside the goal area and near the "goalpost" closest to A1. S3 should be to the side of S4, just outside the other "goalpost.")

After the shot on goal, G2 begins a new round of play, propelling a ball to M2. The exercise continues in the other direction, with the first player A2 joining forces with S1 and S2 for an attack on G1.

The players rotate positions at the coach's discretion.

Variation

The coach may wish to add defenders to offer passive resistance against the midfielders and/or to challenge the strikers.

DEPTH IN DEFENSE

Depth in defense is just as critical as depth in attack. Like the attackers, defenders must also avoid being caught "flat," that is, positioned in a straight line across the field—especially in their own territory. In Figure 2-42 on page 72, for example, the three defenders RB, CH, and LB are caught flat. Should the ball carrier penetrate between RB and CH, by dribbling and/or interpassing with the supporting attacker, all three defenders will be taken out of the play.

Good defense is the result of three basic elements: immediate chase, positioning, and delay. As the attackers progress downfield, the defender nearest the ball carrier must immediately challenge for the ball (*immediate chase*) to slow the play and turn the ball carrier toward the touchline. At the same time, the other defenders must *position* themselves between their defensive goal and the attackers in such a way as to support the challenging defender. Figure 2-43 on page 73 illustrates defensive depth and support for challenger RB. Player CH is in position to cover the supporting attacker, should the ball carrier pass to him; CH is also positioned to cover the ball carrier, should he manage to dribble past RB. Meanwhile, defender LB is racing back to support CH and RB.

Whenever the supporting defenders are not in position at the time the challenging defender man-marks the ball carrier, the challenger must *delay* the ball carrier until he does have support.

The following drills are designed to accustom young players to the above basic principles of depth in defense.

Players: In pairs
Ages: All ages
Playing Area: 10 x 10 yard grids
Equipment: One soccer ball and four markers per pair
Time: Six minutes

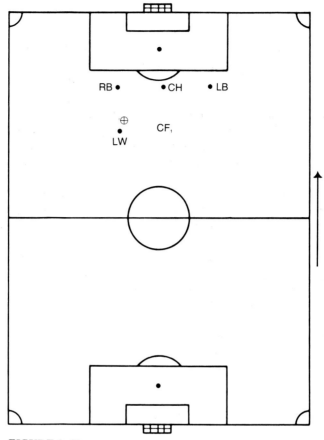

FIGURE 2-42

Markers are placed to establish 10 x 10 yard grids along one touchline. A pair of players, an attacker and a defender, is assigned to each grid. Each attacker has a soccer ball at his feet and stands in one corner of the grid. The defender stands in a corner to the side of the attacker.

On the coach's command, the attackers dribble as quickly as possible across the grid and stop the ball with the foot on any part of the opposite grid line. The defenders give *immediate chase*, trying to tag the attackers before the ball is placed on the line. The players then change roles and continue until each player has completed five rounds as an attacker and five as a defender.

Variation

The grids are increased to 10 x 20 yards, and two additional markers are positioned as in Figure 2-44 on page 74. The attackers must dribble the ball across the

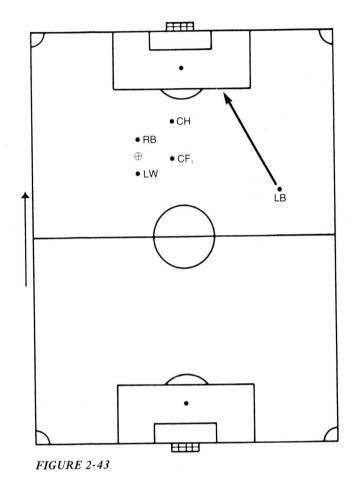

FIGURE 2-43

grid, weave through the markers, and place the ball on the opposite grid line. The defenders begin each round from the same corners as in the original exercise, but resting on one knee. The coach may wish to have the defenders assume other beginning positions that commonly occur in actual game conditions (on both knees, on the stomach, sitting, on their backs, etc.).

Players: In pairs
Ages: All ages
Playing Area: Full field
Equipment: One ball per pair
Time: Ten minutes

The players are divided into pairs (an attacker and a defender) and stand along the center line, half the pairs to each side of the center spot. (See Figure 2-45.) On

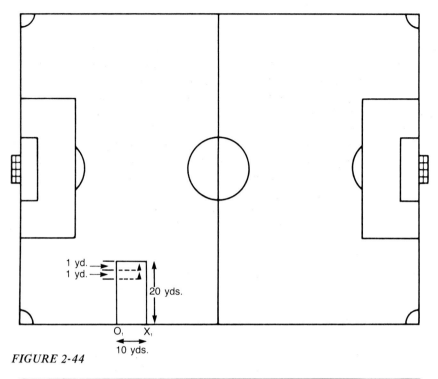

FIGURE 2-44

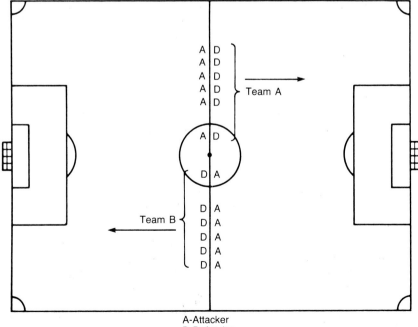

A-Attacker
D-Defender

FIGURE 2-45

the coach's command, the first pair from each side moves into the center circle, staying on the appropriate side of the center line. The two defenders stand with their backs to their respective goals and with their legs wide apart. The attackers face the defenders, standing a yard apart with a ball at their feet.

On command, the attackers pass the ball through the defenders' legs with some weight (power) and immediately chase after and onto the ball. The attackers then dribble downfield at speed and shoot on goal. The defenders, once the ball has passed through their legs, turn and give *immediate chase*, trying to tag the attackers before they shoot.

If an attacker is tagged, he takes push-ups before the two players jog back down the touchline to rejoin their teams and reverse roles.

Variation 1

The defenders face their respective goals, with their backs to the attackers. The ball is once again passed through the defenders' legs, and the game continues as in the original exercise.

Variation 2

The distance between defender and attacker is increased to five yards. The defenders stand facing the attackers, with their feet together. On the coach's command, the attackers pass the ball with power at the feet of the defenders and follow the pass. The defenders jump vertically, allowing the ball to pass. The attackers try to race onto the ball before the defenders can turn, give chase, and attempt the tag.

Players: In pairs
Ages: All ages
Playing Area: 10 x 20 yard grids
Equipment: One soccer ball and four markers per pair
Time: Ten minutes

Four markers are placed to establish each 10 x 20 yard grid along a touchline. A pair of players, an attacker and a defender, is assigned to each grid. The attackers stand along the touchline, facing infield and with a ball at their feet. The defenders stand one yard infield, facing the attackers and with their legs wide apart.

On the coach's command, the attackers pass the ball through the defenders' legs with enough weight (power) that the ball and the attacker will arrive at the opposite grid line at approximately the same time. Once the ball has passed through their legs, the defenders turn and give *immediate chase*. The defenders then try to stay as close to the attackers as possible but do not try to win the ball over.

The attackers control (stop) the ball at the opposite grid line and immediately turn back toward the touchline, ready to go again. The defenders again assume their original positions (one yard from the attacker and legs apart), and the exercise continues as above.

After each series of three round trips, the players rest for approximately forty-five seconds (roughly the time spent in making three round trips). After each three series of round trips, the attackers and defenders reverse roles.

Players: In groups of three
Ages: All ages
Playing Area: 10 x 20 yard grids
Equipment: One soccer ball and four markers per group
Time: Six minutes

Four markers are placed to establish each 10 x 20 yard grid along a touchline (ten yards along the touchline and twenty yards infield). Each group of three players, one attacker and two defenders, is assigned to a grid.

The attacker stands in one corner of the grid with a ball at his feet. One defender (D1) stands in the center of the grid, while the other (D2) stands in a corner to the side of the attacker.

On the coach's command, the attacker dribbles the ball across the grid. The moment the ball is played by the attacker, D1 approaches in an effort to *delay* him. Meanwhile D2 races from his corner to back up D1. Once D2 is in position, D1 challenges for the ball.

The attacker scores a goal by placing the ball on any part of the opposite grid line. A new attacker is designated after each series of three trips, and the game continues until each of the three players has completed three series of trips as the attacker.

Players: In pairs
Ages: All ages
Playing Area: Width of the field
Equipment: One soccer ball per player
Time: Six minutes

The players are divided into pairs, an attacker and a defender. The attackers stand along a touchline, facing infield and with a ball at their feet. The defenders stand approximately two yards infield, facing the attackers.

On the coach's command, the attackers commence to dribble the ball, zigzagging across the field. The defenders backpedal, staying roughly two to three yards in front of the attackers. When the coach blows the whistle, the defenders pounce as if to tackle the ball, only to backpedal and again maintain their distance.

The defenders continue this tactic of *delay* until they reach the opposite touchline. The players then reverse roles and return to the original touchline.

Players: In three teams
Ages: All ages
Playing Area: Half-field

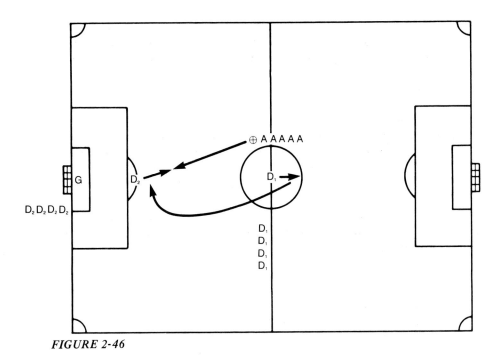

FIGURE 2-46

Equipment: Four or five soccer balls
Time: Twelve to fifteen minutes

The players are divided into three teams. The attackers line up to one side of the center circle, facing the goal. Defending Team 1 stands on the opposite side of the center circle, lined up parallel to the center line. Defending Team 2 lines up at one goalpost. (See Figure 2-46.) One soccer ball is placed in front of the line of attackers and one at the center spot.

On the coach's command, the first attacker in line stands behind the soccer ball, the first player on defending Team 1 (player D1) moves to the center spot, and the first player on defending Team 2 (player D2) moves to the top of the penalty area.

When the coach blows the whistle, the attacker takes one push-up on the ball, stands, and dribbles at speed toward the penalty area. Player D2 moves toward the attacker to *delay* by shepherding him to the side and away from the goal. Player D1 dribbles his ball away from the goal, leaves it at the far end of the center circle, and immediately races to back up D2.

Once D1 is in position, D2 challenges for the ball. If D2 wins the ball over, a goal is scored for the defenders. If the defenders have not won the ball over after twenty-five seconds, time is called and the next attacker and defenders in line take their turn.

Variation

For the start of play, the ball at the center spot is removed and two benches are placed at the part of the center circle away from the goal, roughly two yards apart and both parallel to the center line. Instead of dribbling a ball, defender D1 races away from the goal and hurdles the benches, coming and going, before he can sprint back to support D2.

Players: In five teams
Ages: All ages
Playing Area: Half-field
Equipment: Four or more soccer balls
Time: Twelve to fifteen minutes

The players are divided as equally as possible into five teams. Attacking team A1 lines up to one side of the center circle, facing the goal. A ball is placed on the ground in front of team A1. (Spare balls are left toward the nearer touchline, out of the way.) Attacking team A2 lines up from a corner of the penalty area, extending toward a touchline. (See Figure 2-47.) Defending teams D1 and D2 stand in lines, each parallel to and to either side of the center line, on the opposite side of the center circle from team A1. Defending team D3 lines up from the corner of the goal area nearer team A2.

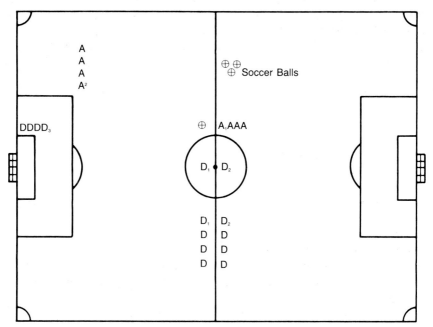

FIGURE 2-47

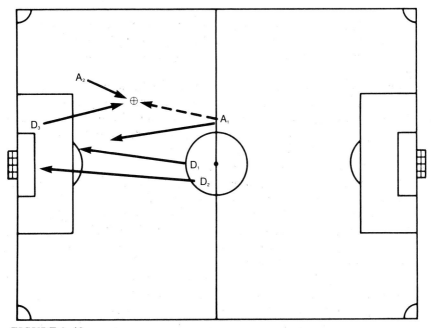

FIGURE 2-48

The first players in line on defending teams D1 and D2 assume a horse and jockey position at the center spot, facing the goal. (For each round of play, D2 players will always be the jockeys.)

On the coach's command, the first player on A1 passes the ball to the first A2, who moves to meet the ball. (See Figure 2-48.) Al follows the pass to support A2. Defending player D1 carries D2 (horse and jockey style) as quickly as possible toward the goal, stopping at the center circle. D2 then dismounts and both defenders race to support D3, who has been *delaying* the attackers. Once the support arrives, the defenders try to win the ball over and the attackers may go for goal.

Each round continues until the attackers score, the defenders touch the ball, or twenty-five seconds have elapsed. Each player then lines up behind his new team: D3 goes to A2, A2 to A1, A1 to D1, D1 to D2, and D2 to D3.

Variation

Defenders D1 and D2 hold a soccer ball between their foreheads, with their hands placed on each other's shoulders. On the coach's command, they move as quickly as possible (one player backpedaling) to the center circle. Once there, the ball is released and the two defenders race back to support D3.

Players: In groups of seven
Ages: Ten and older

Playing Area: Circles, twenty yards in diameter
Equipment: One soccer ball per group
Time: Ten minutes

The players are divided into groups of seven, five attackers and two defenders. The attacking players are positioned in a circle of approximately twenty yards diameter, one with a ball at his feet. The defenders stand within the circle. One of the two defenders is designated as the "chaser."

The attackers are instructed to pass the ball to one another, across the circle or around the circle in either direction. Five consecutive passes completed without an interception by the defenders will count as a goal; one interception equals a goal for the defenders.

During the course of the exercise, the coach blows the whistle, signalling the player receiving the ball at the time to immediately dribble to the nearer penalty area without faking or changing direction. The chaser gives *immediate chase* and attempts to tag the ball carrier before he reaches the penalty area. An additional goal is awarded to the attacker's team if he reaches the penalty area safely or to the defender's team if he tags the attacker.

In the event that the attacker is tagged, he becomes the nonchasing defender and the other original defender becomes the chaser. The original chaser who successfully tagged the ball carrier becomes a member of the attacking team. The game continues until all players have had a turn as the chaser.

Note: Once the attackers have begun passing the ball, the coach should blow the whistle within fifteen seconds for junior players (ages ten to twelve), and within thirty-five seconds for senior players.

Players: In groups of six
Ages: Twelve and older
Playing Area: 10 x 10 yard grids
Equipment: One soccer ball and five markers per group
Time: Six to eight minutes

Four markers are placed to establish 10 x 10 yard grids along one touchline. One additional marker is positioned at the center of each grid.

The players are divided into groups of six, four attackers and two defenders. The attackers stand at the corners, one with a soccer ball at his feet. The two defenders occupy the center of the grid.

The coach instructs the attackers that, on the whistle, they are to pass the ball around the perimeter of the grid, in any direction, trying to complete five consecutive passes, which will count as one goal. If at any time the defenders leave the marker in the center of the grid unprotected, an attacker may shoot at this marker, which will count as two successful passes.

The two defenders try to intercept, as well as to protect the center marker. Either of the two defenders may challenge for the ball or defend the center marker, with the other maintaining proper *positioning* as a back-up. Should a defender intercept a pass, or should an attacker pass the ball at the center marker and miss, the attacker who passed the ball will change roles with a defender.

The game continues until all players have had turns as defenders.

CONCENTRATION IN DEFENSE

Concentration in defense means that the closer the ball comes to the defensive goal, the more concentrated the formation of the defenders. It is almost as if the defenders retreat toward their goal through a funnel, which has its small end at the goal area.

Concentration is most vital when the attacking team occupies a central position in the penalty area. An immediate challenge must be put on the ball carrier,

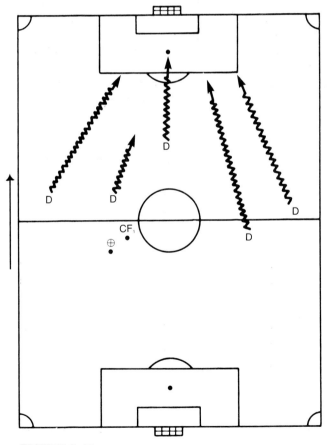

FIGURE 2-49

and supporting defenders must close in on the attackers, narrowing the amount of space available to them and restricting their possibilities for a shot on goal.

In Figure 2-49, the ball carrier is being delayed by defender CF1. Meanwhile, the remaining defenders are in full retreat. Yet, as long as they do not retreat in a straight line across the field, they are playing good defense by applying the principle of concentration. As they approach their penalty area, they become more concentrated, effectively restricting time and space to prevent shots on goal from central positions. (In youth soccer, the greatest percentage of goals and shots on goal come from within the penalty area.)

In Figure 2-50, the ball carrier occupies a central position just inside the penalty area. By applying direct pressure, defender LB forces the ball carrier to make a move. Defenders CH and RB, who have applied the principle of concentration, close in on the attackers to restrict their playing time and available space. Consequently, the attackers must execute perfectly to score.

The following drills are designed to accustom young players to the "funnel" effect for concentration in defense.

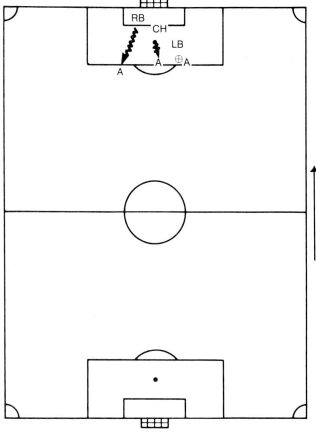

FIGURE 2-50

Players: In groups of eight
Ages: Twelve and older
Playing Area: Anywhere on field
Equipment: One soccer ball and ten markers per group
Time: Twelve to fifteen minutes

For each group of eight players, a pair of markers is placed one yard apart to establish a goal at each corner of a fifteen yard square grid. A fifth pair of markers, again one yard apart, marks a goal fifteen yards from one of the four corner goals. (See Figure 2-51.)

Each group of eight players (five attackers and three defenders) is assigned to a grid and positioned as in Figure 2-51. The defenders are instructed to protect all five goals, especially the goal nearest the ball carrier and, most importantly, the central goal (the one nearest the actual field goal in Figure 2-51). The attackers are to attempt to score on any one of the five goals but, more importantly, are instructed to pass the ball around in an attempt to lull the defenders asleep until they can score on the central goal.

When a goal is scored or when the defenders win the ball over, attacker A1 restarts the game at his original position. Goals may only be scored going forward, i.e., by shooting the ball between a pair of markers in the direction of the regulation field goal.

The game continues for twelve to fifteen minutes, with the players rotating between attack and defense. The coach may wish to introduce additional attackers

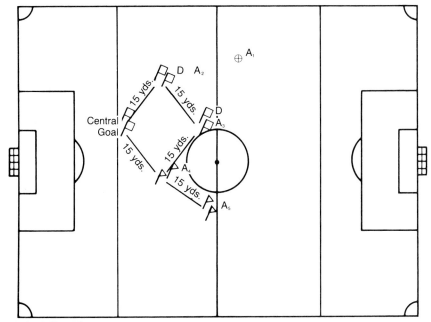

FIGURE 2-51

and defenders or may have the attackers play two-touch soccer (control and pass) in order to achieve greater commitment on the part of the defenders.

Players: One or two groups of ten
Ages: Twelve and older
Playing Area: Half-field per group
Equipment: One soccer ball and five markers per group
Time: Twelve to fifteen minutes

For each group of ten players, a marker is placed on the penalty spot and four additional markers are placed to form a pentagon of roughly ten yards to a side. (See Figure 2-52.) The ten players, six attackers and four defenders, are positioned as in Figure 2-52. Attacking player A1 has a ball at his feet.

On the coach's signal, attacker A1 quickly passes or begins dribbling the ball to open the attack. The attackers score by striking any open marker with the ball. As soon as the ball is in play, the defenders on the center line race back to support their teammates and to close down the spaces leading to the goals.

If the defenders win the ball over, the game is restarted from the center line. Goals may only be scored going forward, that is, in the direction of the regulation field goal.

Players rotate between attack and defense periodically.

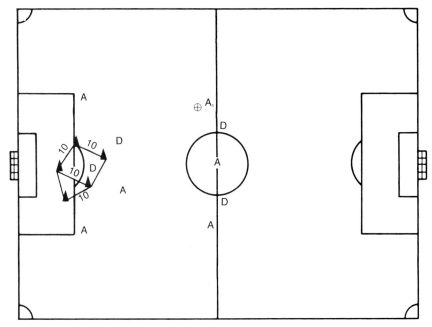

FIGURE 2-52

Variation

A goalkeeper is assigned to the regulation goal. If the defense wins the ball over, the ball is passed immediately to the goalie and all players race back to their original positions. The goalie punts the ball to any attacker on the center line to restart the game.

BALANCE IN DEFENSE

Balance in defense counteracts mobility in attack. If the attacking team interchanges positions in an effort to draw the defenders out of position, the defenders need only switch positions themselves.

In Figure 2-53, the ball carrier is supported by attacking players CF1, CF2, RM, LM, and LW. The defending players obviously have allowed themselves to be

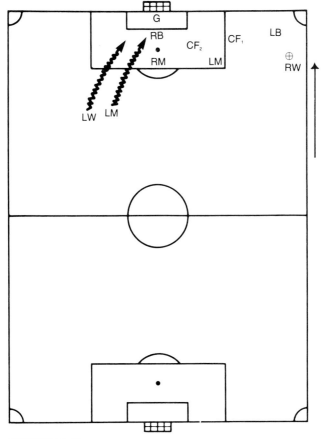

FIGURE 2-53

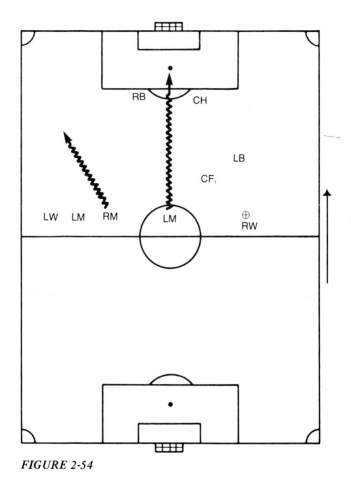

FIGURE 2-54

drawn out of position and are concentrating on the ball carrier. This has created enough space behind the defense for a lead pass to attacker **LW** or **LM** and a shot on goal.

In Figure 2-54, the ball carrier is challenged by defender **LB**, who is supported by **CH**, and defender **RB** has moved into a central covering position. Retreating defensive players **RM** and **LM** move into areas where concentration and balance can be maintained in order to prevent attackers **LW** and **LM** from receiving a cross field pass.

The following drills are designed to accustom young players to maintain balance in terms of defensive positioning.

Players: One or two groups of seven
Ages: Twelve and older
Playing Area: Penalty area for each group

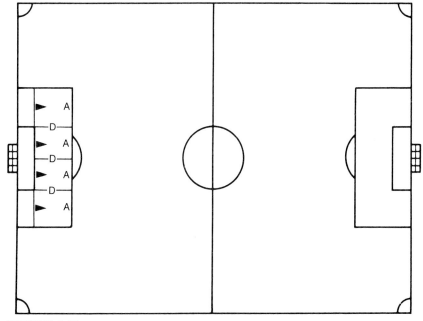

FIGURE 2-55

Equipment: One soccer ball and four markers per group
Time: Twelve minutes

For each group of seven players, four markers are placed at equal intervals in a line extending along the top of the goal area, but running from one side of the penalty area to the other. (See Figure 2-55.) The resulting top portion of the penalty area can thus be visualized as four grids of equal size.

The seven players are divided into four attackers and three defenders. The attackers pass the ball around basketball style and may move through all four grids. The defenders may only move into an adjoining grid if its marker is left unguarded, that is, no two defenders may occupy the same grid at the same time.

On the coach's signal, the attackers commence running and passing the ball around in an attempt to shoot the ball at an unguarded marker. The defenders delay, cover, and challenge for the ball in an effort to make an interception, which will count as a score for them.

Whenever the ball is intercepted or a shot is taken (whether it hits the marker or not), the ball returns to the attackers and the game begins again. Players rotate positions approximately every three minutes.

Variation

Five attackers play against three defenders according to regular soccer rules (no hands).

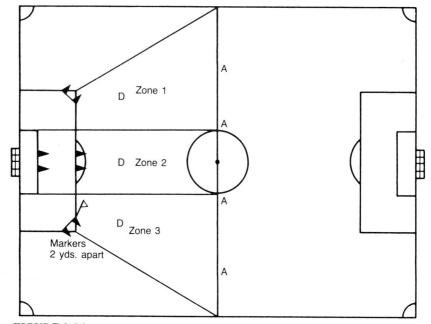

FIGURE 2-56

Players: In groups of seven
Ages: Twelve and older
Playing Area: Half-field per group
Equipment: Eight markers per group
Time: Fifteen minutes

For each group of seven players, half the field is divided into zones and each of four sets of markers is placed two yards apart. (See Figure 2-56.) The seven players are divided into four attackers and three defenders. One attacker will be designated to remain on offense at all times (the designated attacker), ensuring a continuous four versus three situation. A defender is assigned to each of Zones 1 to 3.

The exercise commences from the center line. The attackers play regular soccer and are encouraged to interchange positions in an effort to create an off-balance situation. The attackers score by dribbling the ball through any of the sets of markers.

A defender may only leave his assigned zone to support another defender who is challenging for the ball, and one of the defenders must always be positioned in the central zone (Zone 2).

If the defenders intercept, the ball is passed to the designated attacker, who must then dribble the ball at speed, under pressure from the original attackers, to the safety of the center circle. The game is then restarted.

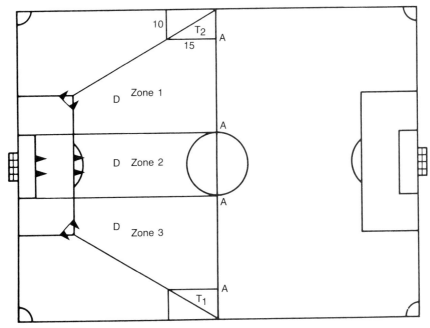

FIGURE 2-57

In the event a goal is scored by the attackers, the game continues until the ball is lost to a defender.

After three minutes, attackers and defenders change roles.

Variation

Target men T1 and T2 are introduced and are positioned in "free zones" near the touchlines. (See Figure 2-57.) If a defender wins the ball over, he immediately passes to either of the target men. Once the ball is received by a target man, he will immediately pass to the designated attacker and the attackers and defenders change roles. The designated attacker may now pass the ball directly across the field to the other target man or may interpass with the new attacking team in an effort to get the ball to the other target man, which counts as a goal.

If there is a breakdown in play, the game is restarted as in the main exercise.

3

Fitness Exercises

Soccer requires forms of fitness that vary from those applicable to other sports. The game demands of its players up to ninety minutes of physical and mental fitness in the specific forms of endurance, strength, mobility, and alertness. While fitness for soccer focuses primarily on ability and on the legs, any fitness program must encompass other aspects, as well.

The twenty exercises presented here represent the most popular and best recognized exercises to be found in coaching manuals. They are taken from an earlier work, *Basic Soccer: Strategies for Successful Player and Program Development* (Allyn and Bacon, 1982). These exercises are designed to develop three of the four aspects of fitness mentioned above: strength, mobility, and alertness. Exercises specifically designed to develop general endurance have not been included, since endurance in young or novice players is best developed through playing.

This section also includes a variety of stretching exercises that can be performed with or without a soccer ball. These exercises should be inserted both before and after practice sessions and should be executed slowly and without stress, in order to avoid muscle pulls and tears.

The following exercises should be rotated, such that each area of the body is worked at each session. The suggested number of repetitions and unit times (the duration of the exercise at each repetition) are offered as guides only. However, based upon experience, the following expectations are reasonable: Players between sixteen and eighteen years of age should be expected to achieve the full number of repetitions and unit times suggested. Players between thirteen and fifteen should achieve at least two-thirds the repetitions and unit times. Players between ten and twelve should achieve one-third the repetitions and unit times. Players under ten years of age should, over the course of the season, achieve the number of repetitions and unit times accomplished by the fittest player at the start of the season.

The suggested number of repetitions and unit times should not be exceeded, in order to avoid fatigue, and each repetition should be followed by a recovery period, during which the players should work on technique, flexibility, and stretching exercises. The length of the recovery period for each of these exercises is three times the work rate.

The unconventional names given some of these exercises, as well as some suggestions for variations on the basic exercises, are for motivational purposes.

IRISH JIG

Equipment: One ball for each one to three players
Unit Time: Thirty-five seconds
Repetitions: Three

The players begin by placing one foot on the soccer ball, then alternate feet at speed.

Effect: Primarily develops the calf muscles.
Suggestions: The players compete for the greatest number of touches within an allowed time. The players rhythm clap as they touch the ball with their feet.

PHOTO 3-1 *Irish jig (feet on and off the soccer ball)*

Recovery Exercise: Hamstring stretch: the players roll the ball around the feet with their hands.

PHOTO 3-2 *Hamstring stretch*

PUSH-UPS ON THE BALL

Equipment: One ball per player
Unit Time: At the discretion of the coach
Repetitions: Ten, increasing to thirty

The players begin in a kneeling position with their hands on the ball. The legs are then extended back and, on command, the players commence to perform pushups on the ball, which must be directly under the chest at all times.

PHOTO 3-3 *Push-ups on the soccer ball*

Effect: Primarily develops the back of the upper arms, chest, and shoulders.

Suggestions: The players are instructed to hold their positions midway through a push-up while the coach tells a story. The coach begins what appears to be a half-hour story but releases the players after approximately seven seconds.

Recovery Exercise: Bilateral quadriceps stretch: the players kneel on the ground and sit back on the heels, with hamstrings fully stretched. The hands are placed as far back as possible, keeping the knees on the ground. Players then return to the upright position. Repeat ten times.

PHOTO 3-4   *Flex and stretch (bilateral quadriceps, hamstrings, and calf muscles)*

PUSH-UPS OVER THE BALL

Equipment: One ball per player
Unit Time: At the discretion of the coach
Repetitions: Ten, increasing to thirty

PHOTO 3-5   *Push-ups over the soccer ball*

The players are positioned on all fours, with a ball directly under the waist. The legs are then extended back until the players are holding in a push-up position. On command, the players move the trunk of the body to the left or right of the ball and lower the chest to the ground. They then push up and repeat the exercise to the opposite side of the ball.

Effect: Primarily develops the back of the upper arms and shoulders.

Suggestions: The players are held in position midway through a push-up for a count of approximately seven seconds.

Recovery Exercise: Groin stretch: the players stand on one leg and raise the other leg, with the knee bent and rotated outward as far as possible. Repeat ten times.

PHOTO 3-6 *Groin stretch*

BALL JUMPING (SIDE TO SIDE)

Equipment: One ball per player
Unit Time: Thirty-five seconds
Repetitions: Three

PHOTO 3-7 *Jumping over the soccer ball (side to side)*

The players stand to the side of the soccer ball. On command, they commence jumping from side to side, making sure that they concentrate on the ball.

Effect: Primarily develops the muscles of the calf and thigh.

Suggestions: If the players experience difficulty in jumping continuously, allow an intermediate jump at either side of the ball until they can complete the exercise properly.

Recovery Exercise: Stretching of bilateral quadriceps, hamstrings, and calf muscles: the players stand with the legs apart and roll the ball by hand in a large circle around the feet. The ball may also be passed through the legs, describing a figure eight.

BALL JUMPING (FRONT TO BACK)

Equipment: One ball per player
Unit Time: Fifteen seconds, increasing to thirty-five
Repetitions: Three

PHOTO 3-8 *Jumping over the soccer ball (front to back)*

The players jump forward over the ball and then back, keeping the feet together at all times.

Effect: Develops the calf muscles.
Recovery Exercise: The players lie on their backs, with one leg raised slightly off the ground. The players then slowly rotate the ankle, clockwise and counter-clockwise. Repeat ten times.

Note: The basic exercise should be conducted at varying parts of the field to prevent wear and tear on the turf.

SOLO TUCK JUMPS

Equipment: One ball per player
Unit Time: At the discretion of the coach
Repetitions: Ten, increasing to thirty

PHOTO 3-9   *Tuck jumps*

The players jump continuously, bringing the knees up high toward the chest.

Effect: Develops muscles of the calf, thigh, and abdomen.

Suggestions: The players count off the repetitions in unison.

Recovery Exercise: The players stand with legs apart and with a ball held to the front in both hands. The arms are fully extended. The players then move the ball around the head, making large circles and occasionally reversing direction.

PAIRED TUCK JUMPS

Equipment: One ball per player (for recovery exercise)

Unit Time: At the discretion of the coach

Repetitions: For each player, three rounds of ten, increasing to three rounds of thirty

The players are paired off, with the first player positioned on all fours. The second player stands to the side of the first player's waist. On command, the standing player tuck-jumps over the kneeling player and then dives or crawls back under him.

PHOTO 3-10 *Tuck jumps (over and under).*

Effect: Develops muscles of the calf and upper thigh.

Suggestions: The players compete for the greatest number of jumps in an allotted time.

Recovery Exercise: Individual ball lifting with the thigh.

SIT-UPS/LEG CURLS

Equipment: One ball per player

Unit Time: At the discretion of the coach

Repetitions: Ten, increasing to thirty

PHOTO 3-11 *Leg curls*

The players lie on their backs with the knees bent, a ball held lightly between the ankles, and the hands locked behind the head. The players then sit up and return to the original position.

Effect: Develops abdomen muscles.

Recovery Exercise: The players lie on their backs with their arms outstretched to the sides. The left leg is lifted over the right and worked up and outward toward the right hand. If possible, the seat should remain in contact with the ground. Repeat ten times.

PHOTO 3-12   *Flex and stretch*

SWIVEL HIPS

Equipment: One ball per player
Unit Time: Fifteen seconds, increasing to thirty-five
Repetitions: Three

PHOTO 3-13   *Swivel hips flex*

The players sit on the ground with arms and legs extended and with a ball held tightly between the ankles. Still holding the ball, the players raise their legs and swing them to the right, at the same time swinging their extended arms to the left. On command, the players reverse the direction of leg and arm movement in a continuous motion.

Effect: Develops muscles of the abdomen and lower back.

Suggestions: This exercise is best performed to popular music or rhythm counting.

Recovery Exercise: The players stand with their legs apart and a ball held in one hand. The ball is then moved around the knees and through the legs, describing a figure eight.

PHOTO 3-14 *Flex and stretch (figure eights around and through legs)*

SQUAT JUMP THRUSTS

Equipment: One ball per player (for recovery exercise)
Unit Time: Fifteen seconds, increasing to thirty-five
Repetitions: Three

PHOTO 3-15 *Squat jump-thrust*

The players assume a squat position. On command, they thrust upward, extending the body before returning to the original position.

Effect: Develops muscles of the upper thighs, as well as activating other muscle groups.

Suggestions: Players are paired off and compete for the greatest number of squat jumps in an allotted time.

Recovery Exercise: Individual ball lifting with the instep only.

PINK PANTHER

Equipment: One ball per player (for recovery exercise)
Unit Time: At the discretion of the coach
Repetitions: Ten, increasing to thirty

Beginning in a sitting position, with hands locked behind the neck, the players raise their fully extended legs and hold. On command, the players bring one knee up to touch the chest, keeping their feet off the ground at all times. The exercise continues, alternating knees.

PHOTO 3-16   Pink panther

Effect: Develops muscles of the upper thigh and abdomen.

Suggestions: This particular exercise is well suited to the tunes "Pink Panther" and "M-i-c-k-e-y M-o-u-s-e." The coach may also wish to slow or speed up the beat.

PHOTO 3-17 *Flex and stretch*

Recovery Exercise: Hamstring stretch: the players sit on the ground, with their legs fully extended and a ball placed near one hip. The ball is then rolled by hand around the feet, behind the back, and back to the original position. Repeat ten times.

LEAP FROG

Equipment: One ball per pair of players (for recovery exercise)
Unit Time: At the discretion of the coach
Repetitions: For each player, three rounds of ten, increasing to three rounds of thirty

PHOTO 3-18 *Leap frog: over (top) and through legs*

The players are positioned in pairs, one standing behind the other and both facing in the same direction. The front player spreads his feet approximately eighteen inches and holds his body in a semi-bent position, with the arms straight and hands placed firmly above the knees. On the signal, the back player leaps over the front player and then dives back through the front player's legs. The exercise is repeated a given number of times before the two players change positions.

Effect: Develops the arms and shoulders of the jumping player, the calf and thigh of the other player.

Suggestions: The players compete for the greatest number of leaps in an allotted time.

Recovery Exercise: The two players stand back to back but approximately a foot apart. The first player, holding a ball, takes it back over the head (similar to the position for a throw-in). The second player reaches back,

PHOTO 3-19   *Flexibility and stretch: overhead (top) and through legs (bottom)*

takes the ball, and passes it through his legs to the first player. The exercise continues as an unbroken series of motions. The distance between players must be such that the players stretch for the ball.

TWISTING PUSH-UPS

Equipment: One ball per pair of players (for recovery exercise)
Unit Time: At the discretion of the coach
Repetitions: For each player, three rounds of ten, increasing to three rounds of twenty

> The players are paired off, with the first player sitting and the second kneeling and lightly gripping the first player's feet. On command, the sitting player twists to the left, performs a push-up, and returns to the original position. The exercise is then repeated to the right side. The players change positions periodically.

PHOTO 3-20 *Twisting push-ups*

Effect: Develops muscles of the arms and shoulders.
Suggestions: The players chant in unison, e.g., "one-and-two-and-three-and-four," etc.
Recovery Exercise: The two players sit back to back but approximately two feet apart. The first player, holding a ball in his hands, twists and passes the ball to the second player, who moves it around his body, twists, and passes

PHOTO 3-21   *Flex and stretch (give and take)*

it back to his partner. The exercise is continued as an unbroken series of movements.

FOOT BOXING

Equipment: None required
Unit Time: Ten seconds, increasing to thirty-five
Repetitions: Three for each player in the pair

The players are paired off, one player lying flat on his back with his hands locked under his lower back. The other player stands at his partner's feet.

PHOTO 3-22   *Boxing partner's feet*

On command, the prone player raises his feet as high as possible, with the legs fully extended, and moves his feet in all directions. The standing player assumes a boxer's stance and tries to slap his partner's feet.

Effect: Develops muscles of the abdomen, calf, and thigh.

Recovery Exercise: Hamstring stretch: the first player lightly holds one foot of the second player, at just below waist height. The second player, now balancing on one foot, slowly lowers his head to the knee of the raised leg, then returns to an upright position. Repeat ten times and change legs.

PHOTO 3-23 *Hamstring stretch*

HORSE AND JOCKEY

Equipment: One ball per player (for recovery exercise)
Unit Time: At the discretion of the coach
Repetitions: For each player, three rounds of ten, increasing to three rounds of thirty

The players are paired off, with one player standing behind the other and facing in the same direction. On command, the back players (the jockeys) jump up onto the backs of the front players (the horses). On a second signal, the horses will raise up on their toes, hold for approximately seven seconds, and then lower themselves.

PHOTO 3-24 *Horse and jockey (toe raisers)*

Effect: Develops calf muscles.
Recovery Exercise: Individual ball lifting with the head.

TWO IN A BOAT

Equipment: None required
Unit Time: At the discretion of the coach
Repetitions: Fifteen, increasing to thirty

The players are paired off, with both players sitting facing one another and with their feet touching. On command, the players grip each others' hands or wrists and commence to rock back and forth. At all times, one player's legs are to be fully extended and the other's bent.

Effect: Develops muscles of the abdomen.
Suggestions: The players chant "in-out" or sing "Row, Row, Row Your Boat."

PHOTO 3-25 *Two in a boat and flex and stretch*

Recovery Exercise: Hamstring and groin stretch: one player stands to the side of the second, lightly holding the nearer foot of the second player. The second player, now balancing on one foot, slowly lowers his head to the knee of the supporting leg, then returns to an upright position. Repeat ten times and change legs.

PHOTO 3-26 *Hamstring and groin stretch*

REACH FOR THE SKY

Equipment: One ball per pair of players (for the recovery exercise)
Unit Time: At the discretion of the coach
Repetitions: For each player, three rounds of ten, increasing to three rounds of thirty

> The players are paired off, with one player positioned on all fours and the other standing at his partner's feet. On command, the standing player lifts his partner's legs and places them to either side of his waist. The standing player then locks his hands under his partner's thighs, and the partner completes a push-up.

PHOTO 3-27 *Reach for the sky*

Effect: Develops muscles of the arms, shoulders, and abdomen.
Suggestions: This exercise can be performed to the sea shanty, "What Shall We Do With the Drunken Sailor," specifically the chorus, "Hooray and up she rises."
Recovery Exercise: The players sit facing one another, with knees bent and the feet touching. The first player, holding a ball and with arms fully extended, lies back on the ground, moving the ball over his head and resting it on the ground. In a continuous motion, this player then brings the ball back to the original position and passes it to his partner, who repeats the exercise. Repeat ten times for each player in a pair.

PHOTO 3-28   *Flex and stretch*

SEAL CLAPS

Equipment: One ball for each pair of players (for recovery exercise)
Unit Time: At the discretion of the coach
Repetitions: For each player, three rounds of ten, increasing to three rounds of twenty-five

The players are paired off, one player lying on his stomach with his arms fully extended to the front. The other player kneels and holds his partner's ankles.

PHOTO 3-29   *Seal claps*

On command, the prone player lifts his upper body off the ground and, keeping his arms extended, claps his hands.

Effect: Develops muscles of the abdomen.
Suggestions: Instead of clapping, the prone player clasps his hands behind his neck.
Recovery Exercise: Working in pairs, the players pass and control the ball with the inside and outside of the foot.

TUG-OF-WAR

Equipment: One ball per pair of players (for recovery exercise)
Unit Time: Thirty-five seconds
Repetitions: Three

The players are paired off and stand facing one another, with their feet touching. On command, the players grip each other's wrists and begin tugging.

PHOTO 3-30 *Tug-of-war*

Effect: Develops muscles of the calf and thigh.
Suggestions: For variety, the players may tug at a soccer ball.
Recovery Exercise: Working in pairs, the players practice throw-ins for distance.

MULE PUSH

Equipment: One ball for each pair of players (for recovery exercise)
Unit Time: Thirty-five seconds
Repetitions: Three rounds for each player in a pair

The players are paired off and stand facing in the same direction, one behind the other. On command, the back player places his hands on his partner's lower back and commences to push. The front player resists.

PHOTO 3-31 *The mule push*

Effect: Develops muscles of the calf, thigh, and upper body.
Recovery Exercise: Working in pairs, the players volley kick and control the ball with the sole of the foot.

4

Fun Games and Exercises

Today's soccer coach has learned to insert fun games and exercises into practice sessions in order to make the sessions more interesting, rewarding, and motivating. Fun games, introduced at the right time, can turn a listless, even frustrated group of players into a highly motivated unit. And although the players are usually unaware of it, these games also incorporate all aspects of the game of soccer—speed, agility, mobility, strength and power, teamwork, mental quickness, and team spirit. As a further advantage, the coach who presents these games enthusiastically, and especially the coach who becomes an active participant, will develop a greater rapport with his players.

The games and exercises presented in this section are among the favorites of experienced coaches. Most are appropriate for younger players or for players of all age ranges. These games are presented first. Games that require the increased skills of older players appear toward the end of this section.

The experienced coach is encouraged to modify these games to fit his players. It is also hoped that these exercises will stimulate the coach to make up some new ones of his own.

MUSICAL SOCCER BALLS

Players: All players
Ages: All ages
Playing Area: Center line area
Equipment: One ball for each two players
Time: Twelve minutes

115

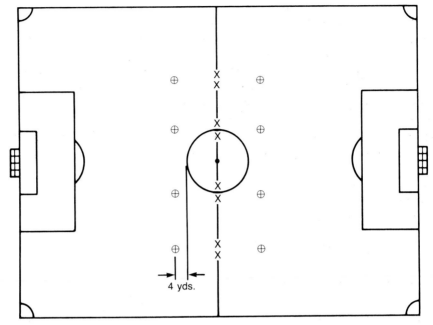

FIGURE 4-1

Soccer balls (one for each two players) are placed in two lines, approximately four yards out from each side of the center circle and parallel to the center line. (See Figure 4-1.) The players line up along the center line in pairs of two, all facing in the same direction.

The players are instructed that, when they hear the command "Go," they are to turn quickly and stand facing in the opposite direction. Upon hearing the command "Soccer balls to your left" (or "to your right"), they are to run with speed in the *opposite* direction of the command and place their right knee (left foot, right elbow, etc.) on a ball. Those players who run in the wrong direction, or who are beaten to the ball, are eliminated from the game.

The coach then removes a pair of soccer balls (one from each line), and the remaining players begin another round. The game is repeated, with the coach continuing to remove balls until only one player remains.

For each round of play, the players are commanded to touch the ball with a different part of their bodies.

Variation

The coach speeds up the command "Go" and every so often, when the players least expect it, gives a false command ("Turn," "Now," "Do it again," etc.). This is done to increase mental alertness, but also for fun. Hopefully the command "Go" will be the only one to which the players respond.

MUSICAL SHIRTS

Players: All players
Ages: All ages
Playing Area: A grid of roughly twenty yards square.
Equipment: Three markers; one ball for each player; shirts or sweatshirts (one for each player minus one)
Time: Fifteen minutes

A grid of approximately twenty yards square is marked off between the center line and a touchline, using the three markers. The players line up around the perimeter of the grid, each with a soccer ball at his feet. (See Figure 4-2.) A number of shirts or sweatshirts (equal to the number of players minus one) are scattered at random within the grid.

The players are instructed to begin dribbling their soccer balls around the perimeter of the grid, all in the same direction. While they are dribbling, the coach gives commands to which they must respond. When they hear the command "Go," all players are to turn quickly and dribble around the grid in the opposite direction. When the command "All in" is given, the players must stay *outside* the grid, while continuing to dribble in the same direction. Upon the command "All out," each player dribbles *into* the grid and places the ball on a shirt with his feet.

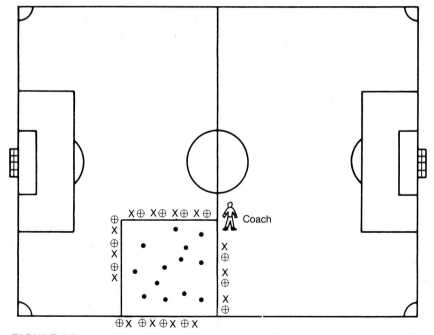

FIGURE 4-2

The coach may have some fun with the players by giving the command "Everyone back out" while the players are within the grid. Of course, "out" means in, and those players responding to this command are eliminated. When the command "In" is given, the players dribble back out of the grid.

During the course of the exercise, the coach removes one shirt for each player eliminated, and the game continues until one player remains. A player is eliminated for failing to respond correctly to the commands or for failing to place his soccer ball on a shirt.

Variations

1. The coach speeds up the verbal commands.
2. The players drag or push the ball with the soles of their feet instead of dribbling.
3. The same exercise is conducted without shirts, with players eliminated only for incorrect responses to commands. In this case, the command "Go" may also be used when the players are inside the grid.

HOLD IT? HEAD IT?

Players: In groups of eight
Ages: All ages
Playing Area: Anywhere on field.
Equipment: One ball per group
Time: Ten minutes

Each group of eight players forms a small circle, approximately six yards in diameter. A coach stands in the center of each circle and tosses the ball to a player while simultaneously issuing one of the following commands: "Head it," meaning to *catch* the ball, or "Hold it," meaning to *head* the ball. The player receiving the ball must respond correctly or be eliminated.

The coach continues around the circle until there is a winner.

Variations

1. Close the circle to half the original distance, thus limiting time in which to react.
2. Substitute commands such as "Chest" or "Catch."

RHYTHM RUNNING

Players: All players
Ages: All ages

Playing Area: Perimeter of the field
Equipment: None
Time: Six minutes

The players jog in pairs around the perimeter of the field, clapping in unison to the beat 1-2-3-clap. The coach, jogging along with them, issues a series of commands in random order. "Go" means to turn and jog in the opposite direction. "Up" means to jump as if to head an imaginary ball. "Down" means to touch the grass with both hands. "Change" means that each pair will exchange positions (the player outside the touchline going to the inside and vice versa). "Check" means to run quickly to the side (away from the other member of the pair) approximately three to four yards and return.

Variations

1. Except for the command "Go," the players are to do the opposite of each command ("Up" means "Down"; "Change" means "Check"; etc.).
2. Upon the command "Go," the front pair of players sprint forward approximately ten yards, turn, and jog to the back of the line. This command is given in conjunction with the others until the original front pair is again leading the group.

TRAFALGAR SQUARE

Players: In four groups
Ages: All ages
Playing Area: Anywhere on the field
Equipment: Two soccer balls; four markers
Time: Twelve minutes

A grid, approximately twenty yards square, is marked off anywhere on the field using four markers. A roughly equal number of players stand behind each of the markers, facing the group diagonally across the grid. Soccer balls are given to any two players at the front of their lines, providing they are not facing each other diagonally across the grid.

On the coach's command, the players with a ball pass it diagonally across the grid and follow their pass, after which they line up at the back of the group opposite. If the two balls collide within the grid, the four active players take push-ups.

The game continues until all players are back in their original positions.

Variations

1. All types of passing, heading, and trapping may be used.
2. Players follow their pass, run around the group diagonally opposite, and

then line up behind the group to the left (right). The game again continues until all players are back to their original positions.

SIMON SAYS

Players: All players
Ages: All ages
Playing Area: Anywhere on the field
Equipment: None required
Time: Ten minutes

The players stand in two parallel lines, facing in the same direction and approximately one yard apart. The coach stands facing the players and leads them through a series of upper and lower body exercises to the command of "Simon says." When the players least expect it, the coach introduces "Sidney says," "Cyril says," or "Sam says." Players responding to any name other than Simon are eliminated.

The game continues until there is a winner.

Variation

All players have a soccer ball and continue to work on upper and lower body exercises, passing drills, and relay competitions—but again responding only to the command of "Simon says."

HORSE AND JOCKEY

Players: Any even number
Ages: All ages
Playing Area: Center circle
Equipment: One soccer ball for each two players
Time: Ten to twelve minutes

The players are divided into pairs and form two concentric circles on the center circle and just outside the center circle. The players in the outer circle (the jockeys) stand with their arms outstretched and their hands on the shoulders of their partners (the horses), who stand with their legs wide apart.

On the command "Go," each jockey will dive through his horse's legs, complete two push-ups, dive or crawl back through the horse's legs, and run (all in the same direction) around the circle and back to the original position. Meanwhile the horses go down on all fours. Once back to the original position, the jockey will sit astride his horse's back. The first pair to complete the exercise is the winner.

Each pair then exchanges positions, and the game is repeated with variations. For example, the jockey now dives through the horse's legs, crawls on all fours around the right leg and back through the horse's legs into the inner circle. The jockey then stands and sprints around the outside of the circle, while the horse gets down on all fours. After completing the circle, the jockey straddles his partner. Again, the first pair to complete the exercise is the winner.

Variation 1

The jockeys take up the same positions as in the previous game, but they now have a soccer ball at their feet. On command, each jockey gets down on all fours and proceeds to push the ball, with his forehead, through the horse's legs. Once through, he stands and dribbles the ball to the outside of and around the circle. Once back to his original position, the jockey picks up the ball and places it between his forehead and his partner's forehead, thus completing the exercise. Jockeys and horses then exchange positions.

Variation 2

Similar to Variation 1, the jockey pushes the ball with his head and follows a figure eight pattern through and around his partner's legs. After completing this maneuver, the jockey stands and dribbles the ball, weaving in and out between all horses in the circle. Once back to his original position, the jockey picks up the ball and places it between his lower back and that of his partner. The pair then attempts to sit. The last pair sitting is assigned push-ups.

Variation 3

Also similar to Variation 1, the jockey now holds the ball between his feet. On command, he sits and with the ball still held firmly between his feet, lifts and moves his body forward and through his partner's legs. Once through, he stands and holds the ball firmly between his thighs. The jockey then can either waddle or "bunny hop" around the outside of the circle and back to his partner. Once back, the jockey takes up a sitting position and completes two sit-ups, with the ball still between his thighs.

THREE BLACK MICE

Players: In groups of three
Ages: All ages
Playing Area: One end of field
Equipment: Three markers
Time: Ten to twelve minutes

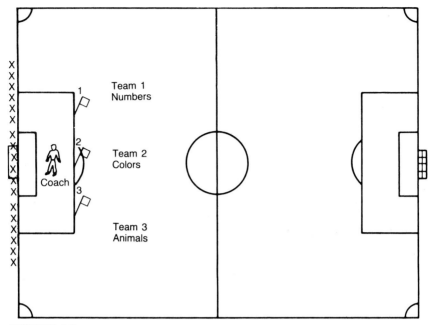

FIGURE 4-3

Three markers are placed along the top of the penalty area as in Figure 4-3. The players are divided into three equal teams.

Each player on Team 1 will be assigned a number, beginning with one, and will stand in line along the goal line, opposite marker number 1. Each player on Team 2 will be assigned a color and will stand in line opposite marker number 2. Each player on Team 3 will be designated as some type of animal and will stand opposite marker number 3.

The coach will call out varying combinations, for example "three black mice." The players designated as the number three, as the color black, and as the mouse will then race out and around their respective markers and back to their original positions. The last two players back will be assigned push-ups.

The races are repeated until all players have had a turn.

Variation 1

Two additional markers are placed in a line behind each original marker, and a soccer ball is placed in front of each original marker. (See Figure 4-4.) To maintain interest, the players exchange names, with the numbers becoming the colors, etc.

At the coach's command, the three appropriate players run to the ball, dribble it between the markers slalom fashion, and return the ball to its original position. The players then sprint back to their respective teams.

The game is repeated until all players have had a turn.

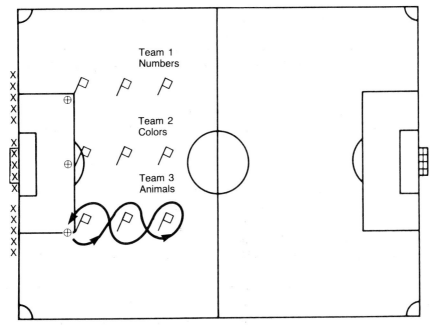

FIGURE 4-4

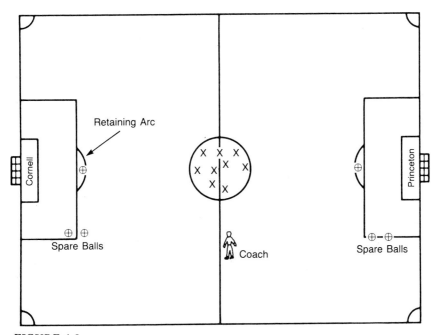

FIGURE 4-5

Variation 2

A soccer ball is placed within each retaining arc, and two spare balls are left at a top corner of each penalty area. (See Figure 4-5 on page 123.) Each goal is assigned the name of one of your opponents.

The players retain their designations as numbers, colors, and animals, and jog around inside the center circle.

The coach calls for three players plus a particular goal (e.g., "six black cows, Cornell"), and the three appropriate players now race to the ball at the Cornell end of the field. The first player to the ball takes a shot on goal; the second player takes one of the spare balls and places it within the retaining arc; the third player retrieves the ball from the goal and places it as a spare. (Goalkeepers may also be inserted for this variation.)

The game continues until all players have had a turn.

Note: When the three players move out of the center circle, the remaining players cease jogging to avoid collisions.

ANATOMICAL RELAY

Players: Four equal teams
Ages: All ages
Playing Area: Between touchline and center of field
Equipment: Two soccer balls per team
Time: Six minutes

Four equal teams of players line up just outside and perpendicular to the touchline. Two soccer balls are placed in front of each team, one ten yards and one fifteen yards infield from the touchline.

The coach instructs the players that, on the command "Go," the player at the front of each line will race to the first ball, kneel, put his hands behind the back, and touch the ball four times: 1) with the forehead; 2) with the chin; 3) with the right ear; and 4) with the left ear. These players will then jump up and race back to the touchline, where they will touch the next player in line with one hand.

The two original players next run backwards to the second ball and 1) sit on the ball and 2) kneel and bend backwards, touching the ball with the back of the head. They then jump up and race back to tag the next player in line, who continues with the same exercise.

The last team to complete the exercise is assigned push-ups.

Variation 1

The players kneel and touch the first ball with 1) the right eye, 2) the left eye, 3) the right knee, and 4) the left knee. At the second ball, the players stand over it and bend one leg such that they can touch it with the inside top of the right and left thighs.

Variation 2

The players kneel and touch the first ball with the right shoulder and the left shoulder. At the second ball, the players place one hand on the ball and run around it five times as quickly as possible.

BLIND MAN'S BALL

Players: In four equal teams
Ages: All ages
Playing Area: Both penalty areas
Equipment: Four soccer balls
Time: Ten to twelve minutes

The players are divided into four equal teams. At each end of the field, two teams stand opposite each other along the outsides of the penalty area. Two soccer balls are placed in each retaining arc.

Four players, one from each team, are blindfolded and instructed that, on command, they are to find their way, with the verbal help of their teammates, to the nearest ball. Once a player reaches the ball, he is to face the goal and shoot to score. (No dribbling allowed.) If the ball does not reach the goal line, the player (again following the verbal instructions of the team) will keep on trying until a goal is scored or the ball passes over the goal line. At this point, the player removes the blindfold, returns the ball to the retaining arc, and races back to blindfold the next player in line.

The game continues as a relay until all players have competed. The two teams accumulating the highest number of goals—one team from each end of the field—then play for the championship.

Variation 1

Only one soccer ball is placed within the retaining arc, leaving two blindfolded players to make their way to the same ball. The first player to touch the ball becomes the attacker and must dribble the ball into the goal to score. The other player becomes the defender and can make a "save" by touching the attacker with a hand or by touching the ball with a foot.

Once a goal or a save is accomplished, the exercise is repeated relay-style until all players have competed. The two teams accumulating the highest number of goals or saves—one team from each end of the field—play for the championship.

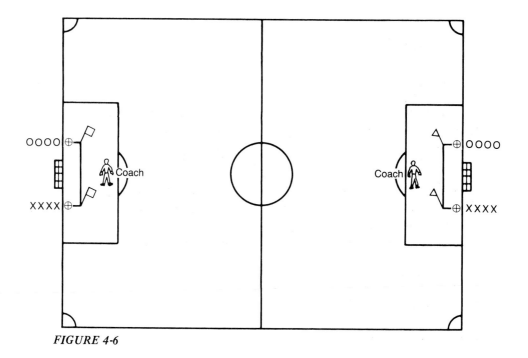

FIGURE 4-6

Variation 2

Markers are placed at the infield corners of each goal area. The four teams line up along the goal lines at the intersection of the goal area lines, facing the opposite end of the field. (See Figure 4-6.)

The first player in each line is blindfolded, and a ball is placed at his feet. On command, the player dribbles the ball out and around the marker and back to his team, following the verbal instructions of the team. The blindfold is then quickly passed on, and the relay continues until all players have competed.

The first two teams to complete the course—one from each end of the field—play for the championship.

CHAIN TAG

Players: All players
Ages: All ages
Playing Area: One penalty area
Equipment: None required
Time: Ten to twelve minutes

Three players are selected to be "chasers" and stand outside the penalty area. The remaining players stand inside the penalty area. On the coach's command, the

PHOTO 4-1   *Chain tag*

three chasers enter the penalty area and attempt to tag as many of the remaining players as possible. As players are tagged, they join hands, until all players have been caught. The chaser who tags the greatest number of players is the winner.

Variation 1

Each of the three chasers has a soccer ball. On the coach's command, the chasers dribble the ball into the penalty area, where they proceed to tag players by shooting the ball (with the side of the foot) at the feet of the other players. Once tagged with the ball, a player sits in the goal area until all players have been caught. The chaser who tags the greatest number of players is the winner.

Variation 2

Play is restricted to a twenty-yard square and all players (chasers included) take up a "crab walk" position. On the coach's command, the three chasers proceed to tag players with their hands or feet. Once tagged, a player teams up with the chaser who caught him and tags other players until everyone has been caught.

The chaser tagging the most players is the winner.

Variation 3

The three chasers stand inside the penalty area. The remaining players line up along the top of the penalty area. The coach instructs the players that when he calls out a number, they must respond with the following actions: 1 = hopping on the right foot; 2 = hopping on the left foot; 3 = jumping with both feet; 4 = crab walk.

The players along the penalty area line must attempt to cross through the penalty area to the goal line without being caught. When the coach calls a number, all players (including the chasers) must respond with the appropriate movement as they attempt to tag or evade tags. Any player tagged by a chaser will change places with that chaser.

Players responding incorrectly to a command perform push-ups (and run the risk of being tagged while doing them). The coach may call out more than one number during the course of a crossing.

HOT POTATO

Players: Any even number
Ages: All ages
Playing Area: Center circle
Equipment: Two soccer balls
Time: Ten to twelve minutes

The players are paired off to form two concentric circles, one just within the center circle, the other approximately three yards further out. (See Figure 4-7.) The

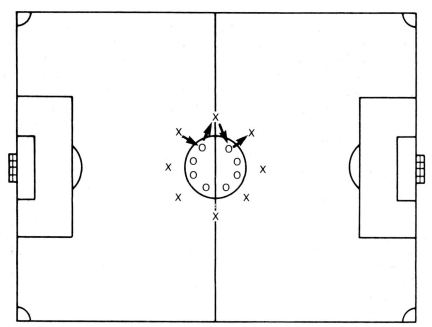

FIGURE 4-7

players should stand so they are fairly evenly distributed around the circles, with the inner circle players lined up to fill the gaps between outer circle players. One soccer ball is held by a player in each circle.

The players are instructed that they are to pass the balls (basketball style) in the direction indicated by the coach. At all times, the outer circles are to pass to inner circle players and vice versa. Whenever they hear the command "Go," the players are to reverse the direction of their passes.

The outer circle players are told they will be designated as "odd," the inner circle players as "even." After a number of "Go" commands, the coach will turn his back and call out "odd" or "even." If he calls "odd," for example, any player in the outer circle who is holding or receiving the ball at the time will be eliminated.

Note: The circles may be made smaller and/or the commands given more frequently to speed up the game.

Variation 1

The balls are passed with the feet for controlling and passing exercise.

Variation 2

A more gradual process of elimination is used, such that an "odd" or "even" player holding or receiving the ball at the time of the coach's call, rather than being eliminated, will rest on one knee and continue to play. If caught a second time, the player will rest on both knees and continue to play. If caught a third time, the player will assume a sitting position, and the fourth time he will be eliminated.

CHANGING OF THE GUARD

Players: In four groups
Ages: All ages
Playing Area: Entire field
Equipment: None required
Time: Ten to twelve minutes

The players are divided into four approximately equal teams and form lines parallel to a touchline. Each player stands roughly three yards from the player immediately in front, in back, and to either side of him. The teams are then assigned numbers from one through four and instructed that, when the coach calls out an odd number, Teams 1 and 3 will change places. The same applies to Teams 2 and 4.

The coach now has the players jog around the field, taking the players through limbering-up exercises. When the players least expect it, the coach calls out a team number. If the number is an even one, the coach may wish to also call out an odd number while the even teams are changing places.

The exercise continues around the field and the fun begins when the players forget that, as they change from one line to another, they acquire a different number. Players responding incorrectly to the coach's calls fall out for push-ups before rejoining the others.

Variations

The coach may wish to insert an additional command that means to reverse direction or may add soccer balls to the exercise to incorporate dribbling practice.

AROUND THE WORLD

Players: All players in pairs
Ages: All ages
Playing Area: Thirty yard square grid
Equipment: Four markers
Time: Twelve to fifteen minutes

Four markers are placed at the corners of a thirty yard square grid around the center circle. Each marker is assigned the name of a country. The players pair off inside the center circle and assume horse and jockey positions.

The coach instructs the players that, for example, when they hear the command "Single to Brazil," all jockeys are to dismount and sprint to the appropriate marker. Upon a command such as "Double to Spain," the horses are to carry the jockeys to that marker. "Double to Spain, changing at Norway" means the horses carry the jockeys to Norway, where they change roles and continue on to Spain.

The last players to arrive at the appropriate marker are assigned push-ups. After each "trip," the pairs return to the center circle and change positions before the game continues.

Variations

The horses carry the jockeys around the circumference of the center circle. Two additional commands are given that mean a) to reverse direction and b) horse and jockey change roles and continue in original direction.

THE ELUSIVE GOAL

Players: All players
Ages: All ages
Playing Area: One penalty area
Equipment: One soccer ball; one rope, twelve to eighteen feet in length
Time: Six minutes

Two players are selected to act as goalkeepers for the movable goal. These players hold either end of a rope, twelve to eighteen feet in length. All other players are divided into two teams.

The coach instructs the players that the game is similar to basketball, except that the team in possession of the ball must constantly be aware of the moving goal. To score, the ball must be propelled by hand underneath the rope, which is held taut to function as a crossbar. The team without the ball tries to intercept, and the two goalkeepers constantly move the rope to prevent broadside shots on goal.

When the ball is shot on goal, the two goalkeepers may quickly lower the rope to the ground, causing the ball to pass over the top. When a shot on goal misses the mark, the ball is passed over to the opposing team.

The coach changes goalkeepers at his discretion.

Variations

The coach may restrict shots on goal to headers or side volley shots. To make the exercise even more demanding, he may require the players to pass the ball according to regular soccer rules, with goals being scored by a player passing the ball under the rope *to a teammate*.

CHICKEN IN A BASKET

Players: In four equal teams
Ages: All ages
Playing Area: One penalty area
Equipment: Four soccer balls; four cardboard boxes, approximately eighteen inches deep
Time: Ten to twelve minutes

The players are divided into four equal teams, which line up just outside and perpendicular to the goal line, facing downfield. A cardboard box ("basket") is placed in front of each team at the top of the penalty area.

The first player on each team holds a soccer ball between his knees and, on command, waddles out to the basket and jumps in, still holding the ball between the knees. The player then makes a clucking sound while releasing the ball into the basket, jumps back out of the box, and races back to tag the next player on his team. The next player races out, makes a two-footed jump into the basket, places the ball between his knees, jumps back out, and waddles back to the team.

The game continues until all players have had a turn. The losing teams are assigned push-ups.

Variation

The players dribble to the box and lift the ball into the box with the instep, after which they race back to tag the next player. The second player races out to the box, stands in it, grips the ball with the feet, jumps back out (still holding the ball), and dribbles back to pass the ball to the next player in line.

SUICIDE RUN

Players: All players
Ages: All ages
Playing Area: One penalty area
Equipment: Four markers; soccer balls
Time: Twelve to fifteen minutes

Four markers are placed to divide the half-field into three equal grids. (See Figure 4-8.) Six players are chosen to be defenders. One defender stands in Grid 1, two in Grid 2, and three in Grid 3. All other players assemble at the end of the penalty area outside Grid 1, each with a soccer ball.

On the coach's command, all players with a ball attempt to dribble to the other end of the penalty area. The defenders attempt to kick the balls away from the ball carriers, but they may not leave their respective grids. Likewise, the ball carriers may not go outside the penalty area.

The ball carriers make as many runs as are necessary to determine a winner. The first player who loses the ball to a particular defender replaces that defender on the next series of runs.

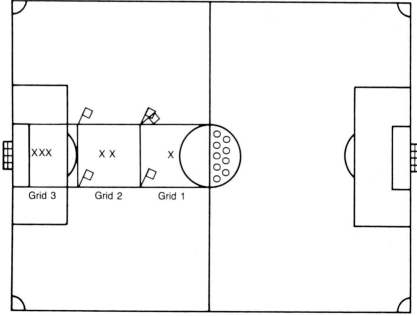

FIGURE 4-8

Variation

The defenders in Grids 2 and 3 hold hands, leaving the ball carriers with even less room to maneuver.

LOG RUN, SNAKE RUN

Players: In two equal teams
Ages: All ages
Playing Area: Length of the field
Equipment: None required
Time: Ten to twelve minutes

The players are divided into two equal teams, which form two lines stretching from one goal line toward the center line, with approximately ten feet between each two players in a line and beginning approximately ten feet infield from the goal line. The players are then instructed to lie on their backs parallel to the goal line.

On the coach's command, the player on each team who is closest to the goal line stands and races to the other end of the line, jumping over his teammates on route as if they were logs. The player then lies down ten feet beyond the last player in line. The next players in line continue the exercise, leap-frog style, until the first player to make the run is again at the front of the line.

On the next series of runs, the "snake run," the players weave between their teammates, slalom style, before lying down ten feet beyond the last player in line.

The exercise continues, alternating log runs and snake runs, from goal line to goal line.

Variation

The players on each team rest on hands and knees rather than lying down. The first player in each line jumps up and sprints down the line, hurdling his teammates, before assuming the same position ten feet beyond the last player in line. On the second series of runs, the first player in each line alternates hurdling and crawling under his teammates.

SINK THE SCHOONER

Players: In two equal teams
Ages: All ages
Playing Area: Anywhere on the field
Equipment: None required
Time: Six minutes

The players are divided into two teams, which form two lines facing each other and roughly ten feet apart. On the coach's command, the first player on each team will take hold of one ankle, pulling it up and back (standing stork fashion). These players then close their eyes, cover them with their free hand, and hop in a complete circle as quickly as possible.

With eyes still closed but not covered, and with ankles still held in position, the players then attempt to tag the next player in line with the free hand. The next player may give verbal assistance as to direction. Once tagged, the next player will repeat the exercise, and so on until all players have had a turn.

The last players in line must find and tag the coach. The first team to complete the exercise will be declared the winner.

Variation

All players on one team hold their ankles, close their eyes, and hop in a circle, after which they must stand for a given period of time. The number of players who maintain their balance and are still standing at the end of the time will constitute that team's score. The other team then attempts to beat that score.

SOCCER HORSESHOES

Players: In groups of four
Ages: All ages
Playing Area: One penalty area
Equipment: One soccer ball per player; two markers for each four players
Time: Fifteen minutes

For each four players, two markers are placed across from one another, one at the top of the penalty area and one eighteen yards beyond towards mid-field. (See Figure 4-9.) The players are divided into teams of two, and two teams are assigned to each pair of markers (to each "range"). A player from Team A, for example, stands with an opponent from Team B at each end of each range. Four soccer balls are placed at one end of each range.

The game commences with one player punting a ball at the opposite marker (with the side of the foot only). The opponent standing next to him does likewise. The first player then punts the second ball, again followed by the opponent. A player who hits the marker directly, with no bounce, scores three points. If there are no direct hits, the player whose ball lies closest to the marker scores one point. A player may use his turn to knock an opponent's ball away from the marker.

After all four balls have been played, the score is tallied and the players at the other end of the range take their turns. The first team to reach a total score of twenty-one is declared the winner.

The length of the range may be increased or decreased, according to skill level.

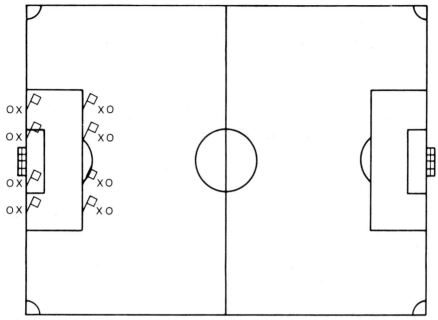

FIGURE 4-9

FOX AND FARMER

Players: All players
Ages: All ages
Playing Area: Center circle
Equipment: None required
Time: Five to ten minutes

The players sit around the circumference of the center circle. Two players are chosen to be the fox and the farmer. On the coach's command, the farmer chases the fox and attempts to tag him within the confines of the center circle. The fox, with agility, speed, and cunning, attempts to avoid the tag. If the fox is tagged within a given time, the two players change roles.

The exercise continues until all players have participated.

Variation

The fox and farmer do not change roles after a tag. Rather, the fox must place one hand on that part of the body tagged while the chase continues (also known as "hospital tag"). The two players continue until the fox is immobilized.

BUZZ, BUZZ

Players: All players
Ages: All ages
Playing Area: Anywhere on the field
Equipment: None required
Time: Three to four minutes

All players stand facing the coach, who instructs them that they are to copy his every action while making a "buzz, buzz" sound. The coach then takes the group through a series of exercises. For example, the coach quickly puts his hands out to the sides and moves the index fingers up and down at speed. The players follow his actions quickly and in unison, "buzzing" to the movement of his fingers.

The exercise continues as the players 1) bend forward as if to touch their toes; 2) extend their arms and describe large and small circles with their index fingers, changing the cadence of their buzzing to slow for large circles and fast for small circles; 3) take up a squat position and pass their hands through their legs from behind; 4) stand with their hands out to the front; 5) bring their index fingers up to and pointing at their armpits.

The coach may wish to add any number of movements to those above, especially movements which are a source of laughs when done at speed.

To conclude the exercise, the coach instructs the players to hold their hands as if ready to clap and to clap every time his hands (held in the same position) pass each other. The coach then proceeds through some fake hand passing motions to catch the players off guard. The coach continues to lure the players by making as if to pass his hands up and down, with an occasional pass to maintain interest. Finally, the coach begins to actually pass his hands, slowly at first and building up to a rapid motion, which means the players will be clapping rapidly. The coach bows as if to acknowledge applause and says "thank you."

POSTMAN'S KNOCK

Players: All players
Ages: All ages
Playing Area: One penalty area
Equipment: One ball per player
Time: Twelve minutes

All players dribble soccer balls, in any direction, within the goal area. The coach (the postman) calls out, for example, "I have a postcard with an eighteen cent stamp." The players must react immediately by dribbling at speed to a line that is eighteen yards long, i.e., to either side of the penalty area. (Six yards = either side of the goal area; twenty yards = the top of the goal area; fourty-four yards =

the top of the penalty area.) After reaching the appropriate line, the players must control the ball and rest it on the line with their foot. (The last player to do so takes one push-up.) The players then return to the goal area to continue dribbling.

After a number of rounds, the coach may call out a combination of stamps: for example, a postcard with six, eighteen, and twenty cent stamps. In this case, the players dribble to the three appropriate lines. Once the players have the ball under control at each line, they must complete two push-ups, two sit-ups, and two tuck jumps before racing back to the goal area. The first player back is the winner.

POPCORN

Players: All players
Ages: Eight and older
Playing Area: Width of the field
Equipment: One soccer ball per player
Time: Ten to twelve minutes

All players stand along one touchline, facing the opposite touchline and holding a soccer ball. On the coach's command, the players commence jogging across the field, tossing the balls gently into the air. On the command "popcorn," the players toss the ball as high as possible, complete a forward roll, jump up, and attempt to catch the ball before it strikes the ground. This continues from touchline to touchline, with the coach substituting various upper and lower body exercises to be completed only upon the command "popcorn."

With younger players, the coach may have them chant "pop, pop" at each toss and catch the ball as they jog, throwing the ball high only on the command "popcorn." This can be fun if the coach teases the players with similar commands, such as "Popeye," "popsicle," "popover," etc., especially if the coach goes through the motion of tossing a ball high while calling out a false command.

Variation

The players pair off, one facing the opposite touchline and one with his back to it. All players facing the opposite touchline are to respond to the command "popcorn," while their partners respond to "Popeye." On the coach's command, all players jog across the field (some will be jogging backwards), with each pair tossing and heading two soccer balls.

When a command is called out, the appropriate players are to immediately turn, sprint five yards, toss the ball high into the air, complete one push-up, and attempt to catch the ball, or bring it under control with some part of the body, before it strikes the ground. After completing the maneuver, these players rejoin their partners and continue across the field, responding only to the appropriate command.

REVERSE TUNNEL BALL

Players: In three or four equal teams
Ages: Eight and older
Playing Area: Penalty area
Equipment: One soccer ball per team
Time: Six to eight minutes

The players are divided into equal teams, which line up, one behind the other, beginning at the goal line and facing downfield. The last player in each line holds a soccer ball. On the coach's command, each player with a ball holds it back over his head (as if for a throw-in), releases it, and attempts to catch it on the first or second bounce by bending at the knees and extending his hands back between the legs. (Players must be standing upright at the time the ball is dropped.)

Once the ball is successfully caught, it is passed to the next player in line, and so on until the player at the front of the line has the ball. This player then runs to the back of the line, the entire line moves forward one position, and the game continues until one team wins by reaching the top of the penalty area.

TAKE IT OR LEAVE IT

Players: In equal groups of four to six
Ages: Ten and older
Playing Area: Grids, 10 x 20 yards
Equipment: One soccer ball per group; markers
Time: Ten minutes

Each group of players is stationed within a 10 x 20 yard grid, and the players are assigned numbers one through (for example) five. For each group, Player 1 is given a ball. On the coach's command, all players jog in any direction within their grid. Player 1 dribbles the ball and looks for Player 2, who approaches Player 1 on the coach's next command. Player 1 has the option of telling Player 2 to "take it" or to "leave it." If he says "leave it," he may continue to dribble for a given period of time (e.g., ten seconds) before allowing Player 2 to take over.

Player 2 then dribbles the ball and looks for Player 3, etc. The game continues until all players have had a turn dribbling the ball.

BULLDOG

Players: All players
Ages: Ten to twelve
Playing Area: One penalty area

Equipment: None required
Time: Ten to twelve minutes

The coach selects one player to be the bulldog, who stands inside the goal area. All other players stand at the top of the penalty area. On the coach's command, the players, except for the bulldog, run for the goal line, trying to avoid the bulldog. The bulldog attempts to catch and hold players for a count of three. Any player caught becomes another bulldog.

The game continues until all players have been caught.

STEAL THE BACON

Players: In four equal teams
Ages: Twelve and older
Playing Area: Full field
Equipment: Three soccer balls; four markers; four benches
Time: Twenty minutes

Two grids of 30 x 44 yards are established by placing markers such that each penalty area is extended infield by ten yards. (See Figure 4-10.) A bench is placed at the center of each resulting thirty-yard line.

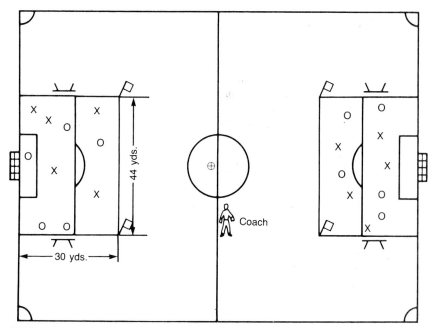

FIGURE 4-10

The players are divided into four equal teams. The players on two teams are assigned numbers (each of the teams having a Player 1, a Player 2, etc.), and two teams are similarly assigned colors. A team of numbers will play a team of colors at each end of the field. A spare soccer ball is placed on the center spot.

The games commence with each team trying to score goals by playing the ball against its opponents' bench. During the course of the games, the coach calls out, for example, "one-yellow." Four players must respond immediately—Player 1 and Player yellow from each end of the field. These four players race to steal the ball from the center spot (the "bacon").

The first player crossing into the center circle is allowed to pick up the ball unchallenged, while the other three players wait outside the circle. The ball carrier has five seconds in which to leave the safety of the center circle before making a run back to his team's grid. Should the ball carrier be tagged on route by an opponent (in the case of a number player, for example, tagged by a color player), all players return to their teams, the ball is placed back on the center spot, and the games continue inside the grids. Should the ball carrier make it back to his grid untouched, an additional goal will be added to his team's final score.

Variation 1

Two balls are placed at the center spot, and the first two players into the center circle attempt to score an additional goal.

Variation 2

The first player crossing into the center circle picks up the ball but must pass it basketball style to his counterpart (the other number or color player) before leaving the center circle. These two players try for either of the grids, continuing to pass the ball while being pursued by their opponents. Should one of these players be tagged or the ball intercepted, the players return to their respective teams with no additional goal being recorded.

SOCCER GOLF

Players: In teams of two
Ages: Fourteen and older
Playing Area: Full field
Equipment: One ball for each two players; nine markers; four benches
Time: Forty-five minutes to an hour

Teams of two are drawn from a hat. To start the game, each team tees off from the top of the goal area and proceeds to marker (hole) 1 with team members

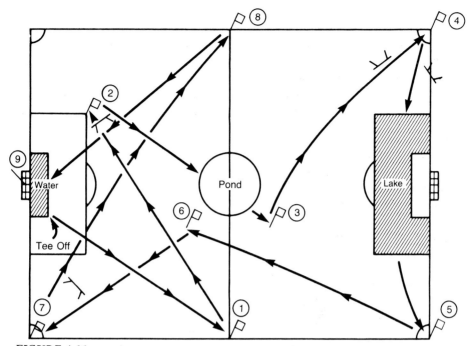

FIGURE 4-11

alternating shots. (See Figure 4-11.) The team playing the ball against the marker with the least number of kicks wins the hole.

Hole 2: A bench (hazard) is placed on its side ten yards in front of the "flag" and in line between the flag and the tee. Players may either chip the ball over the bench or go around it.

Hole 3: The flag is placed five yards beyond the center circle, which serves as a water hazard. Again, the players may chip over the hazard or go around it.

Hole 4: A bench is laid down to either side of and to the front of the flag (sand traps). The players must pass the ball through the opening between benches.

Hole 5: Players must chip over or go around the penalty area (another water hazard).

Hole 6: The flag is placed on the far side of the center circle "pond."

Hole 7: A bench is placed upright, twenty yards in front of the flag. Players must pass the ball under the bench to reach the flag.

Hole 8: No hazards.

Hole 9: The flag is placed inside the goal mouth, with the goal area serving as a water hazard.

Winners may be determined either by the lowest total score or by the number of holes won.

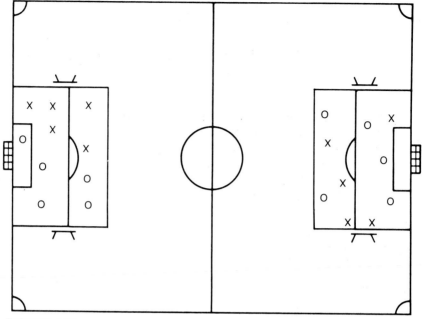

FIGURE 4-12

SOCKBY

Players: In four equal teams
Ages: Fourteen and older
Playing Area: Two grids, 30 x 44 yards
Equipment: Two rugby balls or American footballs; four benches; four markers
Time: Nine minutes per game

Markers are placed in such a way that each penalty area is extended ten yards infield. Benches are placed on their sides at the midpoint of each resulting thirty-yard line. (See Figure 4-12.)

The players are divided into four equal teams (preferably of five players each), and two teams are assigned to each end of the field.

The games commence with a "drop ball" between two opposing players. All regular soccer rules apply, and goals are scored by passing the ball against the opponents' bench. The two winning teams, one from each grid, play for the championship.

Variation 1

Any player with the ball must dribble past at least one opponent before he can pass to a teammate.

Variation 2

The benches are removed and each is replaced by three markers placed at intervals of approximately five yards along the thirty-yard lines. A team scores by ,playing the ball against any one of its opponents' three goals.

SOCCER CRICKET

Players: In groups of six to twelve
Ages: The following drill is presented in three segments, each suitable for a different age range of players
Playing Area: Varies according to player ages; see below
Equipment: One ball and two markers per group
Time: Varies according to player ages; see below

Ages: Ten to twelve. Time: Twenty to thirty minutes

For each group of six to twelve players, two markers are placed as in Figure 4-13. Marker M1 is placed at the intersection of the touchline and the center line; M2 is twelve paces infield from M1 on the center line.

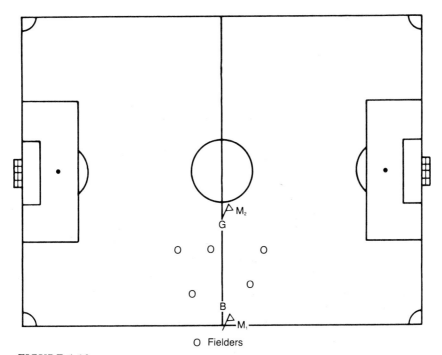

O Fielders

FIGURE 4-13

The batter stands at M1, and the goalkeeper at M2, holding the ball. The remaining players act as fielders.

Play commences when the goalkeeper rolls the ball underhand toward the batter, who instep kicks the ball along the ground, as hard as possible and in any direction. The moment the ball is kicked, the batter runs to touch M2, while the fielder nearest the ball gathers it and full instep volley kicks it to the goalkeeper, who attempts to tag the batter before he can touch the marker.

If the fielders have trouble controlling the ball, the batter may continue running between the two markers for as long as he can safely do so without being tagged. Each touch of a marker, with any part of the batter's body, will count as a score. Once the batter decides to stop running, he will be allowed to return to M1 for another "pitch."

The players rotate positions, with each batter receiving six pitches. The winner is the player who accumulates the highest number of scores.

The coach may wish to place additional restrictions on the fielders, requiring them to control the ball with the sole, outside/inside of the foot, etc.

Ages: Thirteen to fifteen. Time: Thirty minutes

The method of scoring is as above, but the playing area differs. For each group of players, the coach places M1 on the goal line at the midpoint of the goal mouth; M2 is approximately twenty paces directly infield, just outside the penalty area. The batter is again positioned at M1, but the goalkeeper stands at the penalty spot. (See Figure 4-14.)

The goalkeeper throws the ball underhand so it reaches the goal area on the first bounce. The batter sole foot traps the ball and then instep kicks it, along the ground, in any direction within the penalty area. The moment the ball is kicked, the batter again races for M2 and the game continues as above, except the nearest fielder must control the ball with the side of the foot and dribble it to the goalkeeper, who has moved to cover M2.

For variety, the coach may require that the batter full instep volley kick the ball once it has bounced, and that the fielders control the ball with the sole of the foot. If a fielder is successful in executing the sole foot trap, the batter is declared out.

Ages: Sixteen to eighteen. Time: Thirty minutes

The markers are placed opposite one another on the center circle, to either side of the center line. (See Figure 4-15.) Two teams are selected, and a coin flip determines which team will bat first.

The batter again stands at M1 (while his teammates practice dribbling in another part of the field), the goalkeeper stands at M2, and the fielders are stationed at random.

The goalkeeper "pitches" the ball overhand so it reaches the batter at least shoulder high and within the center circle. The batter must head the ball as far and

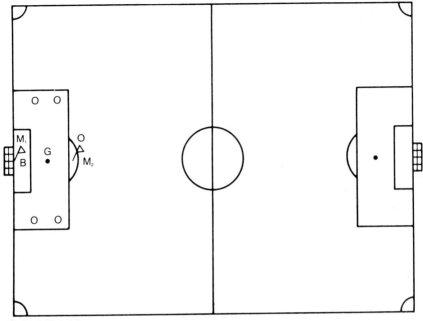

FIGURE 4-14

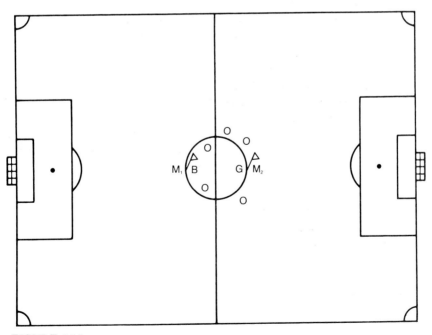

FIGURE 4-15

as high as possible, in any direction, before running to touch M2. The fielder nearest the ball must play it first time (one touch) to the goalkeeper or relay pass it for the goalkeeper, who is covering M2.

Each batter receives six good "pitches," and the team accumulating the highest number of scores wins.

SOCCER BASEBALL

Players: Varies according to player ages; see below
Playing Area: Penalty area(s)
Equipment: See below
Time: Thirty minutes

> *Ages: Ten to twelve, in one or two groups of ten*
> *Equipment: One ball and three markers per group*

For each group of ten players, a marker is placed at each outside corner of the penalty area and one at the midpoint of the retaining arc. The players are divided into two teams of five. After a coin toss to determine which team "bats" first, the fielding team is positioned around the field: one fielder at each marker (base) and two fielders stationed in the outfield (beyond the retaining arc). The

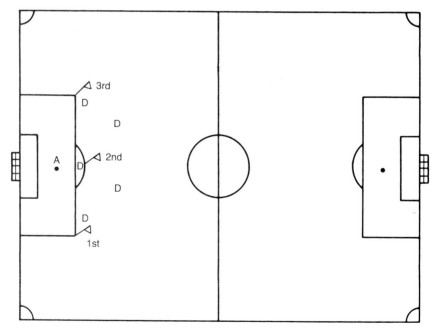

FIGURE 4-16

fielder at second base also functions as the pitcher. The batter stands to one side of the penalty spot. (See Figure 4-16.)

Play commences when the pitcher rolls the ball underhand toward the batter, who must instep kick the ball into the playing area before running to first base. The nearest fielder must control the ball with the sole, inside, or outside of the foot, before gathering it to make a full instep volley kick (out of the hands) to the appropriate fielder. The runner may elect to run beyond first base, depending upon the play of the fielders.

Each batter receives only one pitch, which must be delivered along the ground and at the batter. In the event of a bad pitch, the batter will receive another.

A run is scored each time a batter safely crosses home plate, and the team accumulating the most runs is the winner. A batter must be tagged with the ball for an out, and every three outs the teams change sides. No team may bat for more than five consecutive minutes.

The coach may also wish to require batters to kick the ball with their weaker foot or may require fielders to dribble the ball to the appropriate bases.

Ages: Thirteen to fifteen, in one or two groups of twelve
Equipment: One ball and four markers per group

The bases are positioned as above, with an additional marker placed at the midpoint of the goal mouth to serve as home plate. A coin toss will determine which team bats first. Three fielders are stationed at the bases, with two additional fielders in the outfield and a pitcher at the penalty spot.

Play commences when the pitcher delivers the ball underhand, high enough for the batter to execute a thigh trap, after which the batter may choose to full instep volley kick the ball (no bounce) or to allow one bounce before full instep volley kicking into the field of play. The batter then runs the bases.

The nearest fielder must control the ball using the sole of the foot on the first or second bounce before instep or side foot passing the ball to the appropriate base.

The batter receives only one pitch unless, in the coach's opinion, the pitch was impossible to thigh trap. Either the batter or the marker to which he was running may be tagged for an out. A run is scored each time a batter crosses home plate safely, and the team scoring the most runs wins. No team may bat for more than five minutes at a time.

The coach may also wish to rule that only the pitcher may catch the volley kick (no bounce) for an out; that fielders must control the ball by running through it; and/or that a fielder serve the ball as if making a regular throw-in.

DUTCH TREAT

Players: In groups of seven
Ages: Twelve and older

Playing Area: Grids, 20 x 30 yards
Equipment: Four markers and one ball per group
Time: Twenty minutes

Part 1

For each group of seven players, four markers are placed to establish a 20 x 30 yard grid. Player 1 is provided a soccer ball.

On the coach's signal, all but Player 1 (the ball carrier) jog around within the grid, making occasional sprints, stopping, starting, jumping for imaginary headers, etc. Meanwhile, Player 1 dribbles the ball slowly, faking and weaving, for about fifteen seconds. Player 1 then calls out the next number in sequence (2), at which point the appropriate player moves in to take the ball and dribble in like manner while all other players move about as before.

The exercise continues until Player 7 has had his turn on the ball.

Part 2

The game continues with the ball carrier again calling the next player in sequence, at which point both players move slowly toward one another. Just before the players are about to pass shoulder to shoulder, the ball carrier shouts "take it." The two players then move quickly in opposite directions. The new ball carrier calls the next player, and so on until Player 7 has had his turn.

Part 3

The exercise continues as in Part 2, but at the moment the two players are about to pass shoulder to shoulder, the coach calls out his instructions, either "take it" or "leave it," with the two players reacting accordingly.

Variation 1

The players dribble and pass the ball to the next player in sequence after the latter has executed one of the following maneuvers: a) arc or bent runs around the ball carrier; b) a checked run, i.e., sprinting away from the ball carrier, stopping, turning, and receiving the ball; c) a diagonal run across other players who are moving around the grid.

Variation 2

Player 1 dribbles the ball to begin the exercise. All other players are restricted to two-touch soccer. The coach may wish to make further refinements to this variation, for example: a) Odd numbered players may dribble the ball; even numbers must play one-touch soccer. b) Odd numbered players may make lofted or ground passes only; even numbers must control the ball with the chest, thigh, etc. and are restricted to headers, side volley passes, etc. c) Two soccer balls are provided to Players 1 and 4, who may dribble to start the game before passing to Players 2 and 5, respectively. Players other than 1 and 4 are restricted to two-touch soccer.

Note: It is important that the players call out the numbers. Quick response to the numbers leads to heads-up soccer, speed of execution, and mental quickness.

PIGGIES IN THE MIDDLE

Players: One or two groups of ten
Ages: Twelve and older
Playing Area: Penalty area
Equipment: Four markers and six soccer balls per group
Time: Ten minutes

For each group of ten, four markers are placed to establish a 6 x 10 yard grid extending out from the goal area. (See Figure 4-17.)

Players 2 and 4 stand on the goal side of the grid. Players 1, 3, and 5 stand on the opposite side. A feeder (F) stands approximately five yards from one end of the grid, and a target man (T) stands some five yards from the other end. Three defenders ("piggies") are positioned within the grid.

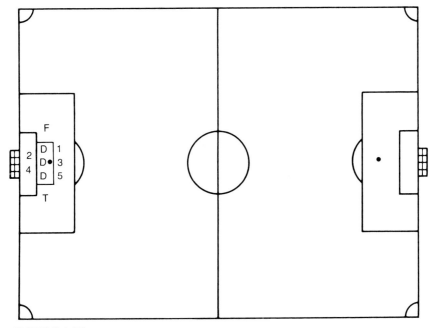

FIGURE 4-17

The exercise begins with the feeder making a proper throw-in to Player 1, who attempts to head the ball over the defenders to Player 2. Player 2 catches the ball and makes a throw-in over the defenders to Player 3, who heads the ball back to Player 4. Player 4 makes a throw-in to Player 5, who then attempts to set up the target man for a head shot on goal.

If a defender intercepts, he replaces the player who last touched the ball. The players rotate positions after each shot on goal.

Variation

A goalkeeper is introduced. Players 1 through 5 may not use their hands, and the target man may head the ball or shoot with the foot to score on the goalkeeper, who may not leave the goal line.

BINGO, BANGO, BONGO

Players: In groups of seven
Ages: Twelve and older
Playing Area: Grids, 8 x 20 yards
Equipment: Four markers and one ball per group
Time: Twelve minutes

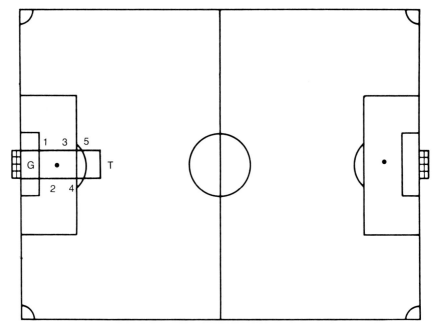

FIGURE 4-18

For each group of seven players, four markers are placed to establish an 8 x 20 yard grid. Players 1, 3, and 5 stand to one side of the grid. Players 2 and 4 stand to the other side. (See Figure 4-18.) A target man (T) is positioned at one end of the grid, facing the goalkeeper at the other end.

Play begins when the goalkeeper underhand tosses the ball to Player 1, who heads it across to Player 2. Player 2 controls the ball and passes it quickly across to Player 3, who must decide whether to control and pass or to make a first-time pass (one-touch pass) across to A4, and so on. Upon receiving the ball, Player 5 sets up the target man for a first-time shot on goal from outside his end of the grid.

Each target man executes four shots on goal before the players rotate positions.

Variation

Two groups of players compete under time pressure. The target man gets only one shot on goal before the players rotate positions (except the goalkeeper). The winning group is the one scoring the most goals within the allotted time. The more quickly a group can execute its preliminary passes, the more opportunities it will have to shoot on goal within the time limit. (The coach may wish to restrict more skilled players to head passes only.)

NUTMEG SLALOM

Players: Any even number
Ages: Twelve and older
Playing Area: Half-field
Equipment: Sixteen markers and two soccer balls
Time: Ten minutes

Eight pairs of markers (placed one yard apart) are positioned as in Figure 4-19, and the players are divided into two equal teams. One team lines up, one behind the other, at each intersection of the goal line and a side of the penalty area. The first player on each team is provided with a ball.

On the coach's signal, the first players dribble to the first gate and pass the ball through. The players themselves run around the outside of the gate to collect the ball on the other side, before continuing on to the next gate.

Once a player has collected the ball beyond the last gate, he may pick it up and sprint back to his team. The next player in line continues the relay, and the first team to complete the course is the winner.

Variations

The gates are placed in a straight line, and the players dribble at top speed. The coach may wish to have the players begin from the center line and finish with a shot on goal. The players may also compete for time and goals scored, with penalty

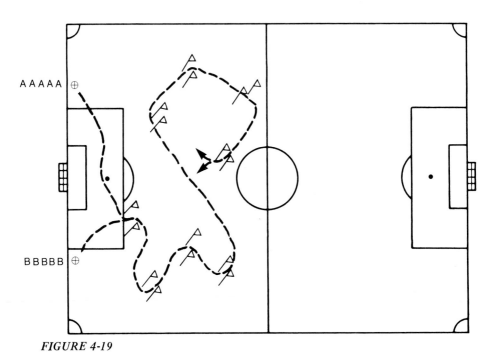

FIGURE 4-19

seconds added to total time for missed shots or, if a goalkeeper is introduced, for saved shots.

SPIN THE PLAYER

Players: In groups of eight to ten
Ages: All ages
Playing Area: Anywhere
Equipment: None required
Time: Five to eight minutes

The players are divided into groups of eight to ten. Each group sits in a small circle, with their legs extended and their feet touching in the middle of the circle. The players then bring their knees up to their chests.

The coach selects one of the smallest (lightest) players to stand in the middle of the circle, and the sitting players tighten the circle around him, extending their arms toward his chest and making sure not to obstruct his feet.

The standing player then stiffens his body and falls toward the sitting players, who support him and spin him around the circle. (Note: There may not be any space between the sitting players, and their arms must be extended at all times.)

PHOTO 4-2　*Spin the player*

Variation

Any sitting player who fails to support the standing player must replace him.

FOX AND HUNTERS

Players:　All players
Ages:　All ages
Playing Area:　One penalty area
Equipment:　One soccer ball
Time:　Twelve to fifteen minutes

The players gather in the penalty area, and the coach forms two teams of "hunters." The coach is the "fox."

The game begins when the coach drops or kicks a ball within the penalty area. The team gaining possession passes it around, basketball style, and attempts to trap the fox by striking him with the ball below the waist, which counts as a goal. The fox is free to move about and hide behind players within the penalty area.

The team without the ball attempts to gain possession in order to score goals themselves. Whenever a goal is scored, the game is restarted as described above.

Variations

1. The teams may be formed according to their regular positions, i.e., forwards versus back players.

PHOTO 4-3 *Fox and hunters*

2. An additional fox may be introduced to the game.
3. The players may be required to play regular soccer, attempting to strike the fox with a normal "shot on goal."

THE NUMBERS GAME

Players: All players
Ages: All ages
Playing Area: Anywhere
Equipment: None required
Time: Four to six minutes

The players are instructed that they must react immediately to the following number commands: 1 = sprint forward; 2 = sprint backward; 3 = sit; 4 = jump for an imaginary head ball. Any player who fails to react immediately, or who reacts incorrectly, takes push-ups.

Variation

Rather than give a number command, the coach performs one of the four movements. The players must immediately react with the opposite movement while calling out the appropriate number for their response.

AROUND THE CLOCK

Players: Twenty-four players
Ages: All ages
Playing Area: Anywhere

PHOTO 4-4 *Around the clock*

Equipment: None required
Time: Ten to twelve minutes

The coach positions twelve pairs of players to correspond to the twelve numbers on the face of a clock, with one player of each pair standing behind his partner. When the coach calls out a time, (e.g., five after two), the appropriate two pairs of players sprint clockwise around the outside of the circle. The last pair back to their original positions take push-ups.

Variations

Instead of racing around the outside of the circle, the two pairs weave through the remaining players in the circle. The coach may also have the two pairs run in opposite directions.

DUCK, DUCK, GOOSE

Players: All players
Ages: All ages
Playing Area: Anywhere
Equipment: None required
Time: Ten to twelve minutes

All players but one sit in a circle, approximately three yards from one another. The remaining player jogs around the outside of the circle, touching the head of each sitting player and, at the same time, saying "duck." When the jogging player comes to a sitting player whom he thinks he can outrun, he touches that player and

PHOTO 4-5   *Duck, Duck, Goose*

says "goose." The jogger then sprints around the circle, pursued by the goose, in an effort to reach the goose's vacated spot before being tagged. If successful, the goose becomes the new jogger. If unsuccessful, the original jogger takes push-ups.

Each player must have a turn as the jogger, and no player may be chosen as the goose more than once.

Variation

The players stand in a circle with their legs spread. After touching the goose, the jogger tries to reach safety by crawling through the legs of any standing player before being tagged.

CROWS AND CRANES

Players: All players
Ages: All ages
Playing Area: Entire field
Equipment: None required
Time: Eight to ten minutes

The players are divided into two teams, the "crows" and the "cranes," which sit in two lines approximately two yards to either side of, and parallel to, the center line. Each player sits directly opposite an opponent in the other line. When the coach calls out a team name (e.g., crows), the appropriate players race for the safety of the nearer penalty area before being tagged by their opponents (in this case, the cranes).

PHOTO 4-6 *Crows and Cranes*

Each chasing player attempts to tag the player who was sitting directly opposite him. Any player tagged must immediately kneel and wait to be counted. The team which tags the most players in an equal number of runs is the winner.

Variation

The coach may have the players begin in a position other than sitting (flat on the back, on the stomach, etc.).

BOAT RACE

Players: All players
Ages: All ages
Playing Area: One goal area
Equipment: None required
Time: Six minutes

The players line up in four teams at the top of a goal area. The first player on each team sits on the top line of the goal area, facing the goal. The remainder of the players sit behind and lock their legs around the player in front of them.

On the coach's signal, all teams move toward the goal line, using only their hands as "oars." Any team (boat) that breaks apart must immediately join up again or be declared "sunk." The first team getting its last man over the goal line is the winner.

Variation

In this exercise, called "Submarine," the first player on each team lies on his stomach, with arms extended and fingers just touching the top line of the goal

PHOTO 4-7 *Boat race*

area. The remainder of the players assume a similar position behind the team leader but hold the ankles of the player in front of them.

The players move toward the goal line using their elbows and knees, except for the first player, who may use his hands to pull himself. Any team that breaks apart must immediately join up or be declared sunk. The first team to have its leader touch the goal line with his fingers, and with the team in tow, is the winner.

PHOTO 4-8 *Submarine*

PHOTO 4-9 *Walk the line*

WALK THE LINE

Players: All players
Ages: All ages
Playing Area: One penalty area
Equipment: None required
Time: Ten minutes

The players are divided into two teams, and the coach appoints a captain for each. The team captains stand on the goal line, to either side of the goal, facing down the sides of the penalty area. The remaining players line up, one behind the other, at the top of the penalty area, facing their respective captains.

The exercise begins when the first player on each team races to his captain and bends over, lowering his head to waist level. The team captain will then spin the player ten times, as rapidly as possible, before the player tries to walk or run back along the side of the penalty area to tag the next player in line. The exercise then continues relay fashion.

The first team to complete the exercise is the winner. Players on the losing team take ten push-ups.

Variation

After being spun, players must walk or run around the center circle.

5

Suggested Preseason Training Programs

The following preseason training programs, presented by age level, are offered as suggestions only. The programs are based on two assumptions: 1) that the time available for preseason training is limited, and 2) that the players are limited in their knowledge of the game and in their technical and tactical skill levels.

The training programs further assume that the players began their soccer experience while in the seven to nine year age category. Obviously, a coach may be confronted with a mixture of older players who are just beginning in soccer and younger players with experience well beyond their age level. In such a case, the coach may draw from the various programs offered.

Hopefully, even the beginning coach will be able to adapt the following training programs to his group of players. By drawing from the different programs and by placing restrictions on more advanced players in order to make the training requirements more demanding, the coach will achieve maximum development for the individual players.

It should be noted that the indicated length of practice sessions, as well as the number of preseason sessions, are estimates. Deviations in length or number of sessions will call for modifications to the basic training programs.

Player Ages: Seven to nine
Practice Sessions: One hour/once a week
Ball Size: Four

Session 1	*Minutes* (Approximate)
(a) Introduce training sessions.	5
(b) Half-field game; observe for player understanding and application of laws of the game.	10
(c) Introduce and walk through Law 1 (field of play) and Law 3 (player positions).	8
(d) Games (from Chapter 1) to improve understanding and application of Laws 1 and 3; correct players as the games progress.	12
(e) Full-field game (eight versus eight; eleven versus eleven) with and without conditions to bring Laws 1 and 3 into play; note continued individual weaknesses.	15
(f) Fun game (from Chapter 4) to improve individual technical skill (e.g., dribbling), finishing with shots on goal.	10

Session 2	*Minutes* (Approximate)
(a) Introduce training session.	5
(b) Fitness exercise (from Chapter 3).	6
(c) Half-field game; (e.g., eight versus eight; eleven versus eleven); observe for understanding and application of Laws 1 and 3.	8
(d) Introduce and walk through Law 8 (start of play) and Law 10 (methods of scoring).	6
(e) Games (from Chapter 1) to improve understanding and application of Laws 8 and 10.	10
(f) Full-field game with and without conditions to bring Laws 8 and 10 into play; note continued individual weaknesses.	15
(g) Fun game (from Chapter 4) to improve individual technical skills (e.g., instep shooting on goal).	10

Session 3	*Minutes* (Approximate)
(a) Introduce training session.	5
(b) Fitness exercise (from Chapter 3).	6
(c) Half-field game (eight versus eight; eleven versus eleven); observe for understanding and application of Law 9 (ball in and out of play) and Law 15 (throw-ins).	8

(d) Introduce and walk through Laws 9 and 15.   8
(e) Games (from Chapter 1) to improve understanding
     and application of Laws 9 and 15.   10
(f) Full-field game (eight versus eight; eleven versus
     eleven) with and without conditions to bring
     Laws 9 and 15 into play; note continued individual
     weaknesses.   15
(g) Fun game (from Chapter 4) to improve individual
     technical skills (including goalkeeping and finishing
     with shots *at* the goalie).   8

Session 4	*Minutes* (Approximate)

(a) Introduce training session.   5
(b) Half-field game (eight versus eight; eleven versus
     eleven); observe for player understanding and
     application of all laws covered thus far.   10
(c) Introduce and walk through Law 16 (goal kicks)
     and Law 17 (corner kicks).   8
(d) Games (from Chapter 1) to improve understanding
     and application of Laws 16 and 17.   12
(e) Full-field game (eight versus eight; eleven versus
     eleven) with and without conditions to bring
     Laws 16 and 17 into play; note continued individual
     weaknesses.   15
(f) Fun games (from Chapter 4) to improve individual
     technical skills, e.g., dribbling at speed, finishing
     with shots on goal.   10

Player Ages: Ten to twelve
Practice Sessions: Sixty to seventy-five minutes/twice a week
Ball Size: Four

Session 1	*Minutes* (Approximate)

(a) Introduce training session.   5
(b) Ball lifting with the instep, stationary and in slow
     motion.   6
(c) Half-field game; observe for individual weaknesses
     relative to ball control.   10
(d) Small-sided games (see Figure 5-1) with emphasis
     on collecting ground balls and passing with all
     parts of the foot; correct players as the games
     progress.   12

(e) Fitness exercises (from Chapter 3).   6
(f) Full-field game (eight versus eight; eleven versus
     eleven) with and without conditions; note continued
     individual weaknesses.   15
(g) Competitive games finishing with shots on goal.   15

Session 2   *Minutes*
                                                               (Approximate)

(a) Introduce training session.   5
(b) Review ball lifting with instep; introduce thigh
     lifting, stationary and in slow motion.   6
(c) Half-field game; observe for individual weaknesses
     relative to controlling air balls.   10
(d) Small-sided games (see Figure 5-1) with emphasis
     on trapping with the sole and inside of the foot.   12
(e) Fitness exercises (from Chapter 3).   6
(f) Full-field game (eight versus eight; eleven versus
     eleven) with and without conditions; note con-
     tinued individual weaknesses.   15

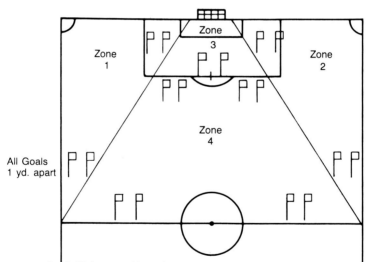

Small-sided games with small goals to improve technical and tactical skills are best
played in those sections of the field that apply to players by assigned position.
For example: In Section 1, a small-sided game (3 v. 3) may contain 3 natural
defenders (right full back, sweeper back, and a right midfielder) playing against three
natural attackers (left wing, striker and a left midfielder).
Note: Many combinations (1 v. 1; 2 v. 1; 2 v. 2; 3 v. 3, etc.) of players by position
may be utilized at the same time throughout the sections.

FIGURE 5-1   Supplementary Training Games by Section (All Ages)

(g) Competitive games involving technical skills covered thus far and finishing with shots on goal.   15

Session 3   *Minutes*
(Approximate)

(a) Introduce training session.   5
(b) Ball lifting with the chest, stationary and in slow motion.   6
(c) Half-field game (eight versus eight; eleven versus eleven); observe for individual weaknesses relative to ball control, especially the thigh trap.   10
(d) Small-sided games (see Figure 5-1) with emphasis on collecting air balls with the thigh.   12
(e) Fitness exercises (from Chapter 3).   6
(f) Full-field game (eight versus eight; eleven versus eleven) with and without conditions; observe for continued individual weaknesses.   15
(g) Competitive games involving technical skills covered thus far and finishing with shots on goal.   15

Session 4   *Minutes*
(Approximate)

(a) Introduce training session.   5
(b) Ball lifting with the head, stationary and in slow motion.   6
(c) Half-field game (eight versus eight; eleven versus eleven); observe for individual weaknesses relative to controlling the ball with the head.   10
(d) Small-sided games (see Figure 5-1) with emphasis on heading.   12
(e) Fun games (from Chapter 4) to improve technical skills.   6
(f) Full-field game (eight versus eight; eleven versus eleven) with and without conditions (hardball, speedball); note continued individual weaknesses.   15
(g) Competitive games involving all types of heading, finishing with headers on goal.   15

Player Ages: Thirteen to fifteen
Practice Sessions: Ninety minutes/twice a week
Ball Size: Five (One ball required for each two players)

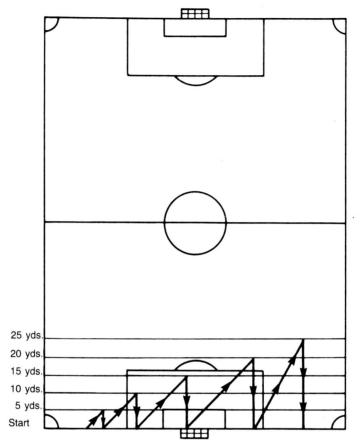

FIGURE 5-2 *Shuttles*

Session 1   *Minutes*
                                                       (Approximate)

Explain and conduct proper warm-up through static
  stretching.   10
Explain and conduct full-fitness training sessions
  through exercises for power and endurance:
  (a) Three series of three shuttle runs from 0–5 yards to
      0–25 yards (35-45 seconds each run), in groups of
      four. (See Figure 5-2.)   6
  (b) Rhythm jog out from a goal line, using the field
      markings; two shuttle runs, each of 0–6, 0–18,
      0–center line, and 0–6 yards. Then jog to opposite
      end of field and repeat. (See Figure 5-3.)   6

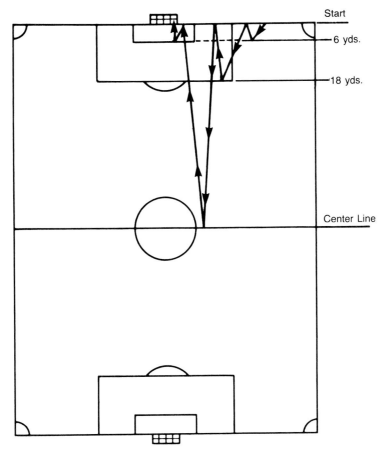

FIGURE 5-3   Half-field Shuttles Example II (b)

(c) Horse and jockey, in pairs, from one touchline to
     penalty area (fifteen yards): A carries B to penalty
     area, then B carries A back. Each player of pair
     completes six runs as horse and six as jockey. (See
     Figure 5-4.)   4
(d) Fun game from Chapter 4 (e.g., Chain Tag).   5
(e) Repeat exercise (a), above.   6
(f) Markers are placed to establish a 12 x 12 yard grid,
     and players are paired off. Each pair of players face
     each other within the grid, one with a ball at his feet.
     The ball carrier attempts to keep possession for a period
     of thirty-five seconds. Each player of a pair takes three
     turns with the ball, with thirty-five seconds rest between.   4
(g) Repeat exercise (a), above.   6

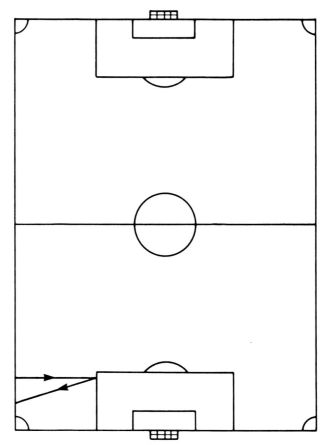

FIGURE 5-4   *Horse and Jockey*

(h) Relay races across the width of the field, in pairs.
     A runs across to B; B runs across and back to A; A
     runs across and back to B. Repeat with B going first.   3
(i) Fun game from Chapter 4 (e.g., Fox and Hunters).   5
(j) Fitness exercises (see Chapter 3): ten squat thrusts,
     ten push-ups, ten sit-ups.   1½
(k) Repeat exercise (a), above.   6
(l) Fitness exercises (see Chapter 3): eight tuck jumps,
     eight half-squat thrusts; eight seal claps.   1
(m) Repeat exercise (f), above.   4
(n) Repeat exercise (c), above.   4
(o) Fitness exercises (see Chapter 3), six of each: leap
     frogs, twisting push-ups, horse and jockey toe raisers.   1½
(p) Repeat exercise (a), above.   6

(q) Fitness exercises (see Chapter 3), four of each: full-
squat thrusts, push-ups, sit-ups.   1
(r) Full-field sprint.   1
(s) Rest interval and conclude with diving headers on goal.   6

Session 2   *Minutes*
                                                            (Approximate)

(a) Static stretching warm-up.   10
(b) Ball lifting.   6
(c) Scrimmage: five versus two in center circle area, with
two-touch restriction and emphasis on mental quick-
ness, technical skills, support, and penetration.   6
(d) Cooper Test Run: 1¾ miles of record number of laps
run in 12 minutes.   15
(e) Fun game from Chapter 4.   6
(f) Half-field game (eight versus eight); observe for
individual and team weaknesses, especially in
tactical skills and in one versus one situations.   10
(g) Explain and demonstrate fundamentals of individual
defense:
  i. Remaining goal side and ball side of opponent.
  ii. Balance on defense and delay as a tactic to gain
    defensive depth.
  iii. Shepherding the ball carrier away from space
    leading to the goal.
  iv. Patience (not committing).
  v. Winning the ball over.   10
(h) Small-sided games to improve individual tactical skills:
(See Chapter 2 and Figure 5-1)
  i. In 12 x 12 yard grid.
  ii. To goal with a goalkeeper inserted.
  iii. To goal with counterattack to a second goal.   20
(i) Full-field game (eight versus eight; eleven versus
eleven) with and without conditions. Note con-
tinued individual weaknesses.   10

Session 3   *Minutes*
                                                            (Approximate)

(a) Static stretching warm-up.   10
(b) Five versus two, restricted to one or two touches.   6
(c) Circuit training for soccer fitness (see Figure 5-5).
Working in pairs, the players complete two full
circuits of eight stations:
Station 1: Pure speed shuttles of fifteen yards.

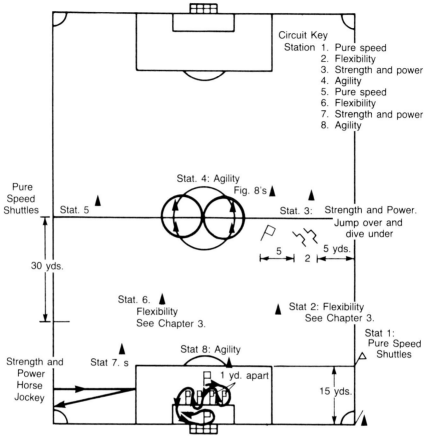

Circuit Key
Station 1. Pure speed
2. Flexibility
3. Strength and power
4. Agility
5. Pure speed
6. Flexibility
7. Strength and power
8. Agility

Stat. 4: Agility
Fig. 8's

Pure Speed Shuttles

Stat. 5

Stat. 3: Strength and Power.
Jump over and dive under

5 | 2 | 5 yds.

30 yds.

Stat. 6.
Flexibility
See Chapter 3.

Stat 2: Flexibility
See Chapter 3.

Stat 1:
Pure Speed Shuttles

Strength and Power Horse Jockey

Stat 7. s

Stat 8: Agility

1 yd. apart

15 yds.

▲ = Cones. One cone at each station bears an index card explaining the exercise.
⊕ = One soccer ball at each station for resting partner.
𝄚 = Flags.
⊓⊐ = Hurdles or benches.

Each player works with a partner for four minutes at each station; at stations 1, 3, 4, 5, 7, and 9 one player works for thirty seconds and then rests for sixty seconds. During rest period player should perform ball lifting sequences or other assigned technical skill. At stations 2 and 6 players may work together.

One minute is allowed players to change from station to station and to prepare for next task.

Competition between players should be encouraged by the coach wherever possible.

FIGURE 5-5 Sample Circuit

    Station 2: Fitness exercises for flexibility (see
      Chapter 3).
    Station 3: Strength/power exercises.
    Station 4: Agility exercises.
    Station 5: Pure speed shuttles of thirty yards.
    Station 6: Fitness exercises for flexibility.
    Station 7: Horse and jockey (see Chapter 3).
    Station 8: Agility exercises.   40

(d) Explain and demonstrate fundamentals of individual
    attack:
    i. Go directly at the defender.
    ii. Beat the defender with speed.
    iii. Do not slow down.   10

(e) Small-sided games to improve individual tactical skills
    (see Chapter 2 and Figure 5-1).
    i. Within a grid.
    ii. To goal with a goalkeeper.
    iii. To goal with a counterattack to a second goal.   15

(f) Full-field game (eight versus eight; eleven versus
    eleven) with and without conditions. Note con-
    tinued individual weaknesses.   10

Session 4	*Minutes* (Approximate)
(a) Static stretching warm-up.	10
(b) Ball lifting in groups.	6
(c) Explain and demonstrate five versus five versus five (see Chapter 2).	20
(d) Fitness test using the training circuit (See Figure 5-5).	40
(e) Fun game from Chapter 4.	6
(f) Half-field game (eight versus eight); observe for understanding of:	15
i. defensive aspects of two versus one.	
ii. offensive aspects of combination play (two versus one).	
(g) Explain and demonstrate:	10
i. defensive aspects of fall back, delay, and patience.	
ii. offensive aspects of support (how, when, and where), give and go passes, check runs, beating the defender by dribbling (isolating the defender).	

(h) Small-sided games to improve individual tactical skills (see Chapter 2 and Figure 5-1).   20

   i. within a grid.

   ii. to goal with a goalkeeper.

   iii. to goal with a counterattack on a second goal.

(i) Full- field game (eight versus eight; eleven versus eleven) with and without conditions. Note continued individual weaknesses.   10

Index